WILL THE REAL YOU PLEASE STAND UP?

WILL THE REAL YOU PLEASE STAND UP?

TEST YOUR PERSONALITY

By

Salvatore V. Didato, Ph.D.

I thank my wife, Dr. Paulette Didato, for her help in editing and proofreading this book, and my son, David Didato, for his valuable help in the technical computer adjustments required to prepare effective copy.

I also wish to honor the memory of the late Dr. Norman Vincent Peale, who over the years provided me with incomparable insights into the human condition.

ISBN: 1494211203
ISBN-13: 9781494211202

This is a sequel to *The Big Book of Personality Tests* (Black Dog & Leventhal, 2003), which has sold over 150,000 copies and is printed in 10 foreign editions. All of the tests and self-evaluations are new and contain research references.

With more than 3,000 personality tests in use today, can anyone doubt that we are certainly the most analyzed creatures on earth? As I explained in my first book, *The Big Book Of Personality Tests*, we are also among the most self-conscious. We never tire of putting our abilities to the test—whether it be at a simple game of Monopoly, a crossword puzzle, a poker session, or an "itch your brain" trivia trip on every conceivable subject from A to Z.

Our craze with hand-held video games that test our speed and savvy on most any topic and now, the iPad which among other features, challenges us to physical contests with wily opponents, certainly show that we have not reached the saturation point as far as tests of our abilities go.

The one topic that commands our unremitting attention is our self. Anything that sheds light on the fascinating mystery of our personality—why we feel and behave as we do, why we do what we shouldn't do and don't do what we should—compels our interest. We want to know what makes us tick.

In this hectic, non-contemplative society, with its many distractions from our inner self, knowledge based on introspection is perhaps the most difficult of all entities to attain. Still our search hasn't diminished a bit. We're ever attuned to how we compare to others, always eager to steal a glimpse of who we are, why we feel and act as we do and, more importantly, what we might become if given the opportunity.

GETTING THE MOST OUT OF THIS BOOK

In planning this book, as I did in my first volume, *The Big Book Of Personality Tests*, I felt that the quiz was the ideal format through which to impart recondite information about the complex subject of personality. Our tests cover 9 domains of living: These are your inner self, your love relations, your family ties, your social sense, your job, your success potential, your mental life and your emotional wellness. They are drawn from some of the finest minds working in those areas. They are culled from research protocols, questionnaires, surveys and clinical experience in fields as diverse as sociology, psychology, psychiatry, and others. Like any tests, they are subject to interpretation and are not the final word, but they have more scientific credibility than those in the runs of an average daily tabloid found at the corner newsstand.

Indeed, many of the questions could very well be part of an interview by a professional doing a personality evaluation; for example some of the following items could be crucial to any psychological profiler:

Do you strongly believe in the death penalty? See Will Virtue Be Rewarded? Chap. 4

Do you often gamble on football games, lotteries, races, or other games? See Is Your Ambition High Enough? Chap. 5

A

Do you believe that a good spanking will correct a child's misbehavior? See Should Kids Be Spanked? Chap. 3

Do you believe if you open up to someone that person will also open up to you? See What's Your Intimacy Index? Chap. 2

You usually dislike lending anything. See How Trusting Are You? Chap. 1

When you are at odds with someone, you don't call him or her, rather, you usually wait until they contact you. See How Do You Handle Disagreements? Chap. 4

You have a tendency to be self-critical. See Is There Anyone Else Like You? Chap. 1

If you are angry with someone is it better to vent your feelings rather than keep in inside yourself? See Do You Rehearse Your Anger? Chap. 4

Do you refrain from eating at night because it is fattening? See Are You Savvy About Your Health? Chap. 8

TEST THE TESTS FOR FUN

To verify a test's conclusions, rate yourself on the trait before you begin. You might ask a friend to join you in your self-ratings and then compare answers. It's possible that if you disagree with your score, it might mean that either you slanted your answers (unintentionally or not) or that you may not have an accurate view of yourself. If this happens, go back and review your responses. Look back on your whole life's history to justify your responses. Ask a trusted friend to check them. Read explanations carefully for important insights.

BE TRUE TO YOURSELF

How accurately this book will really give you a window into your true self depends on your candor. To get the most from a quiz, don't fudge your answers. No one's peering over your shoulder, so be straightforward. It's best to respond without too much deliberation and don't minimize weaknesses or maximize strengths. If you're honest and accurate in your answers, you should come away with a fairly realistic picture of yourself as you truly are. So use a pad and pencil for your answers and get started.

CONTENTS

"'Because it is here'—that's all I can get out of him."

CHAPTER ONE
YOUR TRUE INNER SELF

IS THERE ANYONE ELSE LIKE YOU?

Mind probers who seek to know a person's innermost feelings and attitudes have devised thousands of questionnaires, some straight forward and deceptively simple, others, lengthy, complex and with built- in lie detectors. To establish the usefulness of such tests, the experts sample a sufficient number of people to set up norms against which an individual score may be compared. The tendency of people to give the same answers to test questions is technically called "communaity of response." In other words, people similar to yourself tend to give answers like yours.

So here's a test of ego traits that can help to establish if you belong to the personality majority. After you take the test, read the summary that follows. Some of the conclusions may surprise you, or even irritate you. Psychologists not only have the data to back up their conclusions but also a joker up their sleeve about these conclusions.

Following are ten statements dealing with personality qualities. Answer each one TRUE or FALSE, according to your view of yourself Try to be spontaneous in your answers; don't reflect too much.

QUIZ

1. You have a need for other people to like and admire you. T

2. You have a tendency to be self-critical. T

3. You have a lot of capacity which you have not used to your advantage. F

4. You admit some personality weaknesses, but you are generally able to compensate for them. T

5. You prefer a certain amount of change and variety and become dissatisfied when hemmed in by restrictions and limitations. T

6. You pride yourself as an independent thinker and do not accept other's statements without satisfactory proof. T

7. You have found it unwise to be frank in revealing yourself to others. T

8. Although you appear self-controlled, you really are frequently worried and insecure within yourself. F

9. Security is one of you major goals in life. F

10. At times you are an extravert and sociable, while at other times you are introverted and reserved. T

ANSWERS

Each statement you marked TRUE puts you on the side of the large majority. Each FALSE answer makes you different in at least one trait. It is suggested that seven or more TRUE ANSWERS strongly qualifies you for the personality majority. Five to six and you're probably in the middle, less than four, and you're in the minority.

Here's the percentage of people who are expected to mark each trait as TRUE of themselves:

TRAIT (RATED TRUE)

1 (85%)

2 (82%)

3 (73%)

4 (73%)

5 (91%)

6 (80%)

7 (68%)

8 (61%)

9 (71%)

10 (78%)

SUMMARY

An interesting turnaround was done with the above trait list by Dr. Ross Stagner of Wayne State University. He printed it up and gave it to a special group of people as their own private "personality analysis." Each of them was impressed by how keenly the "analysis" described himself/herself. Over 90% rated it from 'rather good' to 'amazingly accurate'. The surprising thing was that these subjects were sophisticated personnel managers whose business is judging other people.

The joker we mentioned is that all of the traits in the True-False test were not compiled by psychologists but were taken from dream interpretation books and astrology readings.* These traits were tested out by psychologists who found that the large majority believes them to be true of themselves. Nevertheless, charlatans find easy pickings by telling such pseudo-insightful generalities to millions of people and making them believe such statements apply to them distinctively.

So before you accept your next fortune cookie massage as very revealing, keep in mind that it's probably true, too, of most of the folks on your street.

*Incidentally, although generally discredited by practically all scientifically trained persons, astrology and dream forecasts still fascinate and are heartily believed by substantial portions of the population.

WHAT DO YOUR DREAMS REVEAL?

"A dream not understood, is like a letter unopened." This Talmudic saying reflects the ancients' belief that dreams conveyed important messages from either the gods or the devil.

Supposedly, they could diagnose an illness, select a suitable home site or indicate when to start a war. Science finds these superstitions to be bogus and that dreams tell us more about the personality of the dreamer than of the supernatural forces around him.

Serious dream research started about 30 years ago at the University of Chicago Sleep Research Center when Dr. Nathaniel Kleitman discovered that the dream state is accompanied by rapid eye movements (REMs). For the first time in history we had a tangible sign that dreaming was occurring. This single finding alone stimulated more research on dreams than had ever been done before. We now know that dreams, or more important, the notions we have about them, influence our personality.

What do you know about dreams and how they relate to your personality ? Answer True or False to the items ahead to find out.

1. As we grow older our dreams become more pleasant. F

2. Dreams can predict the future. F

3. Dreams can help us to be creative. T

4. Happy dreams suggest a happy person. F

5. We tend to have more unpleasant than pleasant dreams. F

6. Dreams occur by chance and don't have much purpose in our life. F

7. Dreams occur in the deepest part of our sleep. F

8. Since "bad" dreams and nightmares occur when we are not conscious, there's not much we can do about them. F

9. Dreams can help us solve problems. T

10. We can influence our dreams. T

EXPLANATION

1. False. Aging brings on more insecurities about life and hence, more disturbed sleep and dream patterns.

2. False. It may seem at times, that a dream has clairvoyant powers but more likely it's only a reflection of a plan we've consciously thought of. Later, it appears that our dream has predicted or forecast the future.

3. True. Dreams can bring creative inspiration in the things we attempt. Author Robert Louis Stevenson credited a dream for the plot of *Dr. Jekyll and Mr. Hyde*, Richard Wagner conceived the opera *Tristan and Isolde* in a dream and artists Salvador Dali and Paul Klee relied heavily upon dreams and inspiration for their works of art.

4. True. Well-adjusted individuals usually have pleasant dreams but this isn't always the case. Some happy persons tend to repress their anxieties and conflicts and then have disturbed dreams.

5. True. Unpleasant dreams outnumber pleasant ones. In addition, as a dream unfolds, it will become more and more unpleasant. As we grow older our dreams become more disturbing probably because our fears about life increase.

3

6. False. Since we all dream we can safely assume that dreams serve some necessary function, athough we're not exactly sure what it is. If we interfere with a person's dream during REM periods, he will become cranky, impulsive and forgetful. But control subjects roused during non-REM times don't show these changes.

7. False. Dreams come mostly during light and not deep sleep, as commonly thought. The cycle of light to deep slumber is repeated several times a night and we tend to dream more as the night wears on.

8. False. We can sometimes control and direct our dreams. Professor Stephen P. Leberge of Stanford University, writing in *Psychology Today* describes exercises which train people to be aware of their dreams while they are occurring. In these "lucid dreams" it is possible to reason and signal others that we are conscious and to even change the dreams plot if we so choose.

9. True. Experiments on creativity show that "sleeping on a problem" (incubating) sometimes brings a solution. Many creative persons report this. Writers Johann Goethe, Oliver Wendell Holmes and mathematician H. Poincare. Through a dream, Elias Howe gained the final insight which enabled him to invent the sewing machine.

10. True. A number of studies show that we can influence what we dream about. In her book, *"Creative Dreaming"*, Dr. Patricia Garfield of the University of Southern California, shows how American Indians, yogis, and Senoi people of Malaysia regularly create scenarios and direct the action within them to help them make decisions.

SCORE

Tally one point for each correct answer.

8-10 points. High dream IQ. You have a realistic grasp of dreams and human personality.

4-7 points. You have average dream IQ.

0-3 points. You have low dream IQ. Some of your notions about dreams need a rude awakening.

COULD YOU BECOME A COMPULSIVE GAMBLER?

State lotteries as a national institution are here to stay. They, and other forms of gambling are an exciting pastime for some 100 million Americans who legally bet a total of about 30 to 50 billion annually. The Mayo Clinic estimates that for about 12 million bettors, gambling is a vice which threatens their happiness and that of others who share their problem in the family circle.

Neither fame nor money insures that one won't gamble beyond reason, for among the celebs who succumbed to the vice are: Walter Matthau, Mario Puzo, Eddie Fisher, Jack Klugman, Vic Damone, Omar Sharif, and many others.

If you are average, you gamble occasionally but if you go at it heavily you might wonder could this become a compulsive habit? Could it control my life?

The quiz ahead might give a clue to the answer. It is based on questionnaires used by Gambler's Anonymous and other groups to identify the compulsive gambler. Answer Yes or No to each item, then read on for answers.

1. Does your gambling strongly serve to offset a boring lifestyle? U
2. Have you ever gambled to get money to pay off debts? U
3. When you worry or are disappointed, do you turn to gambling as an outlet? U
4. When you lose do you feel a strong urge to gamble again to win back your losses? U
5. Have you ever sold anything to finance your gambling? N
6. Does gambling ever take up time during your normal workday? N
7. After a win, do you feel driven to return again to win more? N
8. Do you gamble with increased amounts of money to become excited? N
9. Do you live close to a betting facility or casino? Y
10. Do you have a substance abuse problem or a mood or personality disorder? Y
11. Do (or did) one or both of your parents have a gambling problem? N
12. Are you a competitive or restless type, a workaholic, or without a strong interest in some life activity? N

EXPLANATION

Little research has been done on pathological gambling. Its victims come from all levels of society. The American Psychiatric Association considers compulsive gambling a disease but this is much disputed by many behavioral scientists who view it as an acquired bad habit based on faulty personality traits. For example, many gamblers have an external locus of control. They don't view their behavior as responsible for wining or losing but usually attribute the results to forces outside of themselves like chance or "lady luck."

Many get their start early in life, (often as teenagers or young adults after they make a "big win" which they never forget. They aren't bothered by statistics which warn that they will lose over 90% of the time. They're prone to magical thinking and believe that they are the exceptions. They are ever alert to signs and omens which point the way to winning and these only fuel the desire to gamble.

Often gamblers hit the dice tables or race track as a diversion to prevent them from coping with other problems, ie a wife, family job, debts, etc. But there are some bright spots in the picture. A number of groups like Gamblers Anonymous, NY, established in 1972 are dedicated to helping those who need it. Probably the largest of these is the Washington Center for Pathological Gambling, College Park, MD. founded in 1978, with Mr. Clark Hudak as its director. Over 1000 persons to date, have gone through their habit-retraining program.

SCORE

Most compulsive gamblers answer Yes to the items above. Take a point for each Yes answer. Our quiz isn't an official test of course, but if you have 5 or more points, you may have tendencies toward becoming a gambler out of control. The higher your score, the more this is likely. For help, contact G.A. in your city to receive help.

HOW TRUSTING ARE YOU?

Interpersonal trust is a necessity of society. Whether seeking a physician, lending money, or forming a club, we must decide whether the risk of disappointment is worth the gain involved. Like it or not, trust in others is a condition for our survival.

Trust exists on many levels. On the material level we trust someone to fix our watch or stereo; on the safety level we trust that other cars won't run a red light or that our bus driver isn't drunk and on the personal level we entrust someone with our love or with intimate disclosures about business or social affairs. All these situations involve varied risk.

Trust is often situational, i.e., you might confide in a stranger at a church meeting more than you would the same stranger at a cocktail lounge.

According to Professor Julian B. Rotter, of the University of Connecticut and others who have researched it, trust appears to be a personality trait like honesty, dominance, etc. It persists and colors our perceptions of the world. Rotter and others have developed tests which distinguish high from low trusters, and our quiz is similar to these. To find your "trust index", answer the items True or False, thinking of people in general and not of specific individuals.

1. When I receive a compliment from a casual acquaintance, my first reaction is to disbelieve it.

2. Most persons would break the law if they thought they could get away with it.

3. People are basically hypocritical.

4. A majority of politicians do not take bribes.

5. Success is more a matter of what you know rather than whom you know.

6. I usually dislike lending anything.

7. Regardless of media hype, people today are just as moral as they were 100 years ago.

8. Most persons who borrow something and return it slightly damaged probably wouldn't mention it to their lender.

9. People don't really face their shortcomings.

10. Most everyone would turn in a wallet with, say, $100 in it.

EXPLANATION

Trusting others is learned. Much of it depends on the nature of our early relationships. If parents, siblings and friends were fair and consistent in dealing with us, if they fulfilled their promises and if they were open and accepting of us, then we most likely will be trusting of others. Inevitably though, our pristine confidence is shaken when we realize that our expectations of people are too unrealistic and, like every child, we go through a confidence dilemma in which we must relinquish our naive perception of the world.

Another side of interpersonal trust has to do with adult life experiences. Suspicious types usually have been emotionally wounded and disappointed (usually in love affairs) and have learned to show caution with others. On this basis, it might be more accurate to say that <u>distrust</u>, rather than trust, is a learned response, for an infant has no previous mental set to be wary of others, but the pain of repeated disappointment will generate the traits of caution and guardedness.

Some interesting questions arise: Can people be taught to distrust? Nazi Minister of Propaganda Josef Goebbels thought so. "Repeat a lie often enough and people will believe it," he intoned. Propaganda psychology is based on this notion and strong distrust between social groups can be achieved by such unrelenting slander.

Is there a gender difference in trust? Studies at Tufts University and elsewhere show that women tend to score higher on measures of generalized trust than men do. To them, people are innocent until proven guilty.

Are high trusters naive as a group? To some degree, they are, concludes Rotter, but the majority of them are not simplistic in their thinking Instead they tend to be no less intelligent or gullible than low trusters. Compared with their opposites, they tend to be happier, more likeable and more dependable.

As we mentioned, interpersonal trust involves risk. and the question will always be: Will the gain outweigh the chance of betrayal or rejection?

Dr. Carl Rogers, founder of the humanist movement in psychology and former director of the Center for the Study of the Human Person in La Jolla, Calif., concluded after much research that realistic trust and acceptance of others usually go along with self-acceptance and are indicators of a well-adjusted personality.

SCORE

Key: 1-F, 2-F, 3-F, 4-T, 5-T, 6-F, 7-T, 8-F, 9-F, 10-T

Take a point for each correct answer.

8-10 points. You are a trusting person who accepts others as you see them. But be careful. You may have to guard against the tendency to be somewhat gullible and naive.

5-7 points. You have a balance between trust and caution. Usually you tend to give the benefit of the doubt in judging others.

0-4 points. You are more guarded and suspicious than most of us. You were not born this way, to be sure. Your acquired distrust is based on unhappy experiences which cause you to analyze other's motives fairly closely.

ARE YOU A VIDEO FREAK?

Do you get turned off when your TV is turned on, but keeping watching anyway? If so, you could be a TV compulsive.

In its 53rd annual television report, the AC Nielsen survey company reveals that an average household watches TV 33 hours per week. This is the highest frequency ever reported. Other surveys show that most viewers believe the tube lacks quality.

The push button joy box brings opinion, entertainment and news as well as nonsense to millions who, although they complain about it, continue to wearily watch its offerings with somnolent indifference.

Sociologists R. Frank of the Wharton Business School and M. Greenberg of Booz, Allen and Hamilton, business consultants, conducted a 4 year study of case histories and found that addicts have certain traits in common. These are found in the quiz ahead. What's your viewer rating?

Answer each item using this scale: 1 Hardly ever, 2 Occasionally, 3 Often

1. After my favorite program is over, I remain unselectively watching TV for an hour or more.

2. When I have spare time, I look at the tube.

3. My conversations with friends revolve around shows we have seen.

4. I prefer watching the news than reading about it.

5. I watch more than 20 hours per week.

6. About 75% of the programs I see in any one month, are fictional.

7. When friends visit, we spend part of the time watching TV.

8. I watch TV at definite times during the day or evening regardless of the programs being offered.

9. I view TV well past my bedtime.

10. I watch for long periods (2-3 hours) without a break.

EXPLANATION

Viewing TV unselectively is like eating anything placed before you without judging whether it's good or bad health-wise. Obviously, the beneficial reasons for watching TV are numerous. As a teaching medium, educators find that it is a proven powerful tool.

But are you making the unwarranted assumption that if some is good, more is better?

Being exposed to long stretches of inferior programming could prove psychologically and intellectually damaging. Consider these caveats:

1. Over dependency-The desire to initiate our own unique plan for a creative construc- tive pursuit could be dampened, as we yield to easily digested planned activity by TV characters.

2. Social withdrawal- Some of us might get excessive vicarious experiences through the actions and beliefs of others. This indirect participation in life can stultify social adaptability and weaken our desire to interface with others.

3. Shrinking critical judgment- Constant exposure to the attitudes and opinions of others, neatly packaged and delivered to us, could create a kind of intellectual laziness to read, study and dig out answers for ourselves.

4. Short-run expertise- Some programs, but not all, often serve up to us brief, succinct, summary statements, which might condition us to a kind of dilettante learning on a varied

number of subjects. We become experts superficially with no in-depth understanding of a topic.

Addicts view TV not as a medium for gaining useful information and a grasp of the world, but more in terms of passive entertainment.

SCORE

Tote up your points and find your view rating below:

8-15 points. Low dependency

16-21 points. Moderate dependency

22-30 points. High dependency

WHO WATCHES TV?

Apparently it has different strokes for different folks. Frank and Greenberg discovered some surprising facts like:

Male blue-collar workers watch TV sports less than do most groups of women. Watching pro-social programs tends to defuse aggression in viewers.

The biggest audience for soaps is early teenage girls.

Adolescent boys tend to favor shows which poke fun at male authority figures.

Those who watch the tube the least, consist of very religious males.

No matter what your reason for viewing video, there is a limit. Being a prisoner of a very limited range of programs narrows your perspective and deprives you of a variety of experiences necessary for a healthy mind set. If you do watch, be sure you stick with quality shows which promote mental stimulation and growth.

TRUE OR FALSE, WHAT YOU DON'T KNOW WON'T HURT YOU. (ARE YOU A BLUNTER OR MONITOR?)

Coping with dread is very much an individual matter. Imagine two people about to undergo similar surgery. One asks the surgeon what he will do and how he will do it, what pain is expected, what the after-effects will be, etc. The other prefers not to ask any questions and distracts himself by making a cell phone call and flipping through a magazine in the waiting room. Patient number one is known as a monitor, one who seeks information about the upcoming stressful event; the other is a blunter, who tunes out and would rather remain pleasantly unaware of the future.

Question: Who will show less stress or discomfort during and after the procedure, the monitor or the blunter?

Professor Suzanne Miller of Temple University, finds that the answer to the question depends on a number of factors She has done considerable research on which types of personality can best endure future anxiety in stress situations.

When it comes to coping with angst, her work shows that most persons fall clearly into the two categories above, blunters and monitors. Lest you think that it's best to "let it all hang out" and that the fact-gathering monitor is better off than the oblivious blunter, you might be wrong.

Dr. Miller concludes from almost a decade of study that this may not always be the case.

To find if you tend to be a monitor or a blunter, take the quiz ahead then read on for answers. *

QUIZ

Vividly imagine that you are on a plane 30 minutes from your destination when it unexpectedly goes into a deep dive then suddenly levels off. After a while, the pilot announces: "There is nothing wrong folks but the rest of the ride may be rough, please continue to enjoy the movie."

Check all the statements ahead, which might apply to you.

I would:

1. Carefully read the information provided about safety features in the plane and make sure I knew where the emergency exits were.

2. Concentrate on making small talk with the passenger beside me.

3. Watch the movie to the end, even if I had seen it before.

4. Call for the stewardess and ask her exactly what the problem is.

5. Order a drink or tranquilizer from her.

6. Listen carefully to the engines for unusual noises and watch the crew to see if their behavior is out of the ordinary.

7. "Blow off steam" to the passenger beside me about what might be wrong.

8. Settle down, read a book or magazine or write a letter.

For items 9 and 10, imagine that you are having dental work done. Answer true or false, which of the following would you most likely do?

9. Ask the dentist precisely what he was going to do.

10. Perhaps ask one or two questions then try relaxing to ease any pain.

SCORE

Items 1, 4, 6, 7 and 9 are reactions patterns of monitors 2, 3, 5, 8, and 10 are those of blunters. If you checked at least 4 monitor reactions or at lease 4 blunter reactions, then that is your characteristic coping style with anxiety situations.

EXPLANATION

How much should a doctor tell a patient before treatment or surgery? Will knowing about an upcoming event create more harm than good? Miller concludes that much of it depends on the patient's personality. Extreme vigilant types who compulsively ask questions about what they face may create more worry (and physiological upset) than necessary to deal with the event. She found that high blood pressure patients are twice as likely to be monitors than blunters. On the other hand, strong blunters may miss important facts, which could reduce their angst and help them to cope better.

After studying hundreds of subjects, she finds that one style is no more effective than the other and each person seems capable of sensing just how much pressure he can tolerate. How well a person fares in an unpredictable event depends upon the "fit of his characteristic style to the individual situation." This means that if you are a vigilant, it's probably best for you to get information (but not an excessive amount) and if you are an avoider, to receive little information about your circumstance.

Monitors do best when they get what they seek and blunters do best when left in the dark. These coping styles are usually set by the age of 6 years.

In times of extreme stress it is best to tune out our fear and to deny that things could go wrong. Putting the matter out of mind usually promotes relaxation, a necessity for most emergencies. Dr. Richard Lazarus, University of California, Berkeley, followed over 60 pre-surgery patients and found that avoiders had fewer post-operative complications (i.e., infection, bleeding, fever, etc.) and were discharged sooner than vigilants.

So what to conclude from all this? When faced with danger ask yourself: Will the information I gather help me to do something constructive for myself or am I powerless to do anything about the outcome?

*This quiz is a copyrighted test of Dr. Miller who granted permission to use it here.

DO YOU SING BEFORE BREAKFAST?
(HOW HAPPY ARE YOU?)PART 1

Happiness is a constant goal of everyone, yes, even of psychologists. Should you think these professionals are concerned only with the tragic and morose aspects of behavior, guess again. They also probe for traits of the truly happy man or woman.

One of many such studies were done by the Institute for Social Research at the University of Michigan, famous for its national polls. The questions asked were similar to those on our quiz. To find what your happiness quotient is, answer each item as objectively as you can and tally a 1, 2 or 3 for your answer.

1. Most of the things I do are: boring (1), interesting (3), in between (2). 3

2. Life: doesn't seem to give me a chance (1), is usually lucky for me (3), is in between (2). 3

3. My general level of stress is: high (1), low (3), in between (2). 3

4. I am: worrisome (1), pretty secure (3), in between (2). 2

5. I am generally: a restless type (1), an easy-going type (3), in between (2). 2

6. I have often: felt very lonely (1), had many friends (3), in between (2). 2

7. I usually feel: dissatisfied with my accomplishments (1), satisfied with my accomplishments (3), in between (2). 3

8. As far as how I handle decisions goes I feel: incompetent (1), quite competent (3), in between (2). 2

9. I am generally displeased with my neighborhood (1), happy with it (3), in-between (2).

10. Overall, I am: discontent with my friends (1), pleased with them (3), in-between (2).

EXPLANATION

How do you judge such a subjective state of mind? Is it a balance between desires and satisfaction, a baby, a sports car, a "thing called Joe?" There are many definitions.

The ISR judged the sense of well being on six quality of life scales, which are the bases of our quiz. These are: outlook on life (items 1&2), stress level (3&4), positive vs. negative feelings (5&6), feelings of personal competence (7&8) and overall satisfaction (9 & 10).

On reviewing the ISR results, *Psychology Today* raised an interesting question: are there differences in happiness in various parts of the nation? To learn the answer, PT combined the ISR data with that of the National Opinion Research Center and came up with distinct regional differences in feelings of life-joy over the United States.

The country was divided into 9 regions and those who made the highest scores on happiness were found to live in the central section of the country, i.e., Minnesota, the Dakotas then directly south to the Gulf of Mexico. Those who scored lowest resided in the north central and middle Atlantic states, i.e., NY, N.J., PA, IN. MI, WI. and OH.

Does happiness change from generation to generation? Professor Angus Campbell of ISR, reviewing the data says it doesn't. Life satisfaction has changed only slightly in the past 2 generations. In 1951, for example about 35% said they were very happy and today, about 30% declare they have a high sense of psychological well-being.

SCORE

Because of the complexity of our subject, the quiz is only an estimate of the trait we examine here. Total up your points and consider the following:

10-17 points is low and indicates a strongly dissatisfied sense of being.

18-22 points is about average for life contentment.

23 or higher points reveals an abundance of joy in living.

(Now follow up by taking the next quiz to validate your score here.)

ARE YOU TRULY HAPPY? PART 2

Life joy is that elusive state of mind that all of us pursue but not everyone attains. It's hard to say what happiness is. To some athletic teen, it means making the team, to some it's having a baby, and to some seniors, it means a productive retirement.

But although happiness is, in the final analysis, a subjective state, psychologists have identified certain clues which signal its absence.

If you've every wondered how you compare with others, on living the good life, the quiz ahead might shed some light on the subject.

Answer "yes" or "no" to the items, then read on for explanations:

1. I tend to lose my temper with little provocation
2. My contentment depends a lot on doing things with people
3. I tend to daydream about happy times, past and future
4. I enjoy my job.
5. I often feel under stress
6. I think much cheating goes on where the honor system is used
7. I prefer reading fiction to non-fiction
8. I eat or drink too much
9. I usually sleep soundly
10. I have an above- average tension level

SCORE

People who are happy and well-adjusted tend to answer the items as follows:

1. No; 2. Yes; 3. No; 4. Yes; 5. No; 6. No; 7. Yes; 8. No; 9. Yes; 10. No.

A score of 5 is average. The closer your score is to 10, the happier you are, compared with others.

EXPLANATION

We don't know how happy we are compared to others because we lack standards against which to make a judgment. One of the most direct ways to gauge a person's joy is to know how much satisfaction he or she gets from work or play. Some of these pleasures may be simple, like taking a swim or visiting a friend, others are more involved, like getting a job promotion, or winning an award.

The late Theodore Lentz, director of the Character Research Association in St. Louis, Mo., conducted extensive surveys on happiness. He found that happy persons tend to have certain characteristics, i.e., they are even-tempered, free from loneliness and inner tensions, (items 1, 5, 10), enjoy their work, keep occupied and interested in things when alone, and do not overindulge themselves with food or drink (2, 4, and 8). When their goals are thwarted, they do not resort to daydreams for consolation (3). When they do dream, it happens during a night's sound slumber (9). When they read they can depart from the reality of factual events and enjoy someone else's imagination by reading fiction (7). They feel relatively secure about their world and tend to trust others (6).

Dr. Lentz found a connection between conservatism and happiness. A conservative person is inclined to be content with things as they are and accepts change gradually. Presumably such satisfaction with the *status quo* tends to increase contentment and produce less frustration.

He also found that wealth or material goods don't necessarily bring joyous living. Lest you believe that money will launch you on the royal road to bliss, some wealthy persons were found to be strongly discontent with their lives.

John G. Shedd, noted Chicago businessman and benefactor of the Shedd Aquarium, once pithily summed it up when he answered the question: How much money would it take to make a man truly happy? The famed tycoon thought a moment, then retorted wryly, "Just a little bit more."

DEEP DOWN, ARE YOU BASICALLY SHY?"

If you've ever felt diminished in the presence of others, you're not alone.

From time to time, all of us, yes even the most aggressive, experience situations which arouse feelings of inadequacy. It's estimated that about 120 million Americans can be called shy: That's about 40% with 60% in far eastern nations.

No matter where they live, shy persons have certain behavior in common. They:

1. Are more prone to being victims of confidence games.
2. Do not receive job promotions as often as non-shy persons do.
3. Are often depressed, anxious and lonely.
4. Are usually self-critical.
5. Do not make good leaders or salespersons.

If you've ever felt that, down deep, you are a dyed-in-the-wool shy soul, take the quiz ahead. Answer true or false, then read on.

1. I feel uneasy even in familiar social settings.
2. I usually find it hard to accept compliments.
3. I'm not too relaxed when it comes to socializing with strangers of the opposite sex.
4. I try to avoid places which might compel me to be very sociable.
5. Being introduced to someone makes me feel nervous.
6. I usually try to avoid speaking with persons unless I know them.
7. When with others, I tend to listen much more than I talk.
8. It would make me "up tight" to speak with a very attractive person.
9. I would feel pretty tense if approached by a police officer.
10. I would feel very uneasy if someone I casually knew revealed a personal problem to me.

Shyness is nothing to feel shy about. It has been called the universal malady. It is usually acquired (copied) from family members. A shy mother usually engenders her response patterns in her children, more strongly in her daughters than her sons.

Research by Dr. Philip Zimbardo of Stanford University, finds that shyness is a state of mind, a reaction pattern induced largely by the society in which we are raised. Some are traditionally reserved and reticent (Japan and India). while others are bold and assertive (Red China and Israel). Children of shyness-generating societies often are not encouraged to express their feelings and opinions openly. They are rewarded (praised, complimented, etc.) for inhibiting their assertive feelings, especially toward authority figures such as parents, teachers and bosses.

SCORE

Our items are similar to those used on social avoidance and shyness tests. The more True answers you gave, the shyer you tend to be. Consider that a score of 4 or less is average.

MEASURING SHYNESS IN INCHES

Our feelings about someone determine how physically close we'll get to them. That is, if we love someone, chances are we will move close as we interface with them. But if we feel shy or fearful with them, we'll tend to create more distance with them.

Such was the topic of study for Professors. B. Carlucci of the University of Indiana and A. Webber of California State University. Their task was to see if shy persons, compared with those who were not shy, tend to keep a wider comfort zone between them and strangers.

As you might guess, the shy do keep their distance. They prefer a distance 8 inches farther away (33 1/2 inches on average) than did the less shy who move in to about 25 inches. The difference increased by 12 inches when the shy persons met someone of the opposite sex.

DO YOU HAVE "HARDENING OF THE CATEGORIES?" (PREJUDICE: THE UNADMITTED TRAIT)

Prejudice is the oldest form of man's inhumanity to man. No matter what our rung on the social ladder, there is always someone below who can be scapegoated for our displeasure.

When poet Robert Burns wrote that it's a gift to see ourselves as others see us, he probably wasn't writing about prejudiced folks, for they seldom realize (or will admit) that they hold biased views of others. The fact is, no one is completely free of bias, no matter how noble one's intention.

Ahead is a quiz drawn from research. To find if you might harbor some stereotyped views of others, answer the items as follows:

Disagree (1); Agree somewhat (2); Agree (3). Then read on for answers.

1. I tend to lose my temper easily with people who rub me the wrong way. 2
2. I am strongly traditional and conservative in my attitudes. 1
3. I grew up in a harsh and punitive family environment. 1
4. I often wish for great psychological power and strength. 1
5. I lean toward severe punishment and a generally hard line of discipline for public offenders. 1
6. Once I make my mind up, it isn't easy to change it. 2
7. I tend to be strongly suspicious of the motives of others. 1
8. I know very little about people of ethnic groups other than my own. 1
9. Some ethnic groups are much more trustworthy than others. 1
10. When people ask me a question, it gripes me to have to say I don't know the answer. 3
11. I have been told that I have low self-esteem. 1
12. My friends know it doesn't take much frustration to get me angry. 1

ANSWERS

The story goes that a young child comes in from play to ask her mother: "Mom, what was the name of those people I was supposed to hate?"

The incident reflects what is largely at the root of human bias, namely, interpersonal influence. If you look at each quiz item, you'll notice that many of the traits described can be traced to learning within the family circle.

Professor Gordon Allport of Harvard University, a pioneer on studies of prejudice, noted that prejudiced personalities have a tendency to cling to past solutions and not try novel ones. They are inflexible thinkers and are hesitant to say, "I don't know." They like clear-cut views of things and are intolerant of ambiguity. Literally, they are narrow-minded. Allport's conclusions have been verified many times by other researchers.

SCORE

Total your points. Though this isn't an official test, consider that your score means the following:

12-18 points. You're mature and relatively free of prejudice.

19-26 points. You have an average degree of bias about others. But there's room for improvement.

27-36 points. Move over Archie Bunker. You are likely to have too many prejudices about others. Try to learn more about those you may dislike. You might discover that they struggle with the same life problems as you do.

REDUCING BIGOTRY

Can prejudice be overcome? Yes. Examine your own beliefs and ask: have I outgrown some faulty notions I've had about others? One possible antidote for intolerance is for opposing groups to join together in doing something cooperatively. Studies of integrated housing and of racially mixed platoons in the Armed Forces show that both sides became more mutually accepting than before they interfaced. But not all cooperative ventures have such a desired effect.

Much will depend upon whether the parties involved feel unpressured about integrating and whether they are given equal status.

COULD YOU BE TAKEN FOR A SUCKER?

To preserve the purpose of the test ahead, answer true or false to the items <u>now</u>, then read on for explanations.

1. If I had to choose, I would prefer a career helping the poor than being in the military.
2. If I could go back in time, I'd rather meet Shakespeare than Columbus.
3. I often think that people take advantage of my good nature.
4. I usually comply with all kinds of requests from friends and family.
5. It's almost always better to be neutral than to start an argument.
6. I usually will stop to help or take home an injured animal.

7. I have a tendency to buy from or make donations to people who come to my door.

8. Tears often come to my eyes in sad movies.

9. I usually would not object if someone pushed in front of me in a line.

10. I would not complain to a restaurant manager that the smoking of a nearby patron annoyed me.

11. I prefer novels to political non-fiction.

12. I usually brood more than I should over being criticized socially.

EXPLANATION

Empathy is the capacity to feel and think the way another person does—to put us, so to speak, in his shoes. It is the basis for all social relations. But sometimes it can be overdone. Like any other human trait, empathy can be so intense as to be called soft-heartedness.

If you've ever felt like you are a pushover in the face of pressure put on you by others or if you have ever felt like a sucker for a "sob story," the quiz ahead may help you. It will indicate the possibility that you are not objective enough in dealing with others.

Extensive work was done at Georgetown University in Washington, D.C., and by Mark H. Davis of the University of Texas on the trait of empathy. It was found that those with too little of this characteristic wind up having difficulty relating to others. On the other hand, those who are too sympathetic may possess traits which reflect personal shortcomings. It can come from being highly suggestible, easily influenced and low on self-confidence. Or it may also stem from a lack of solid personal values and a clear sense of right and wrong. Some softhearted persons long to be accepted, and fear being rejected or criticized if they are not agreeable to everyone.

Superabundant love and concern for all mankind is possible in some individuals but it's a rare pattern indeed. For many, this behavior may be largely naive; for others, it may reflect a deeply spiritual calling. Our quiz taps only a few aspects of this complex personality trait.

SCORE

Most persons will answer true to some items, but "softies" will tend to answer true to most of them. Consider that the higher your score is over 8, the more you tend to fall in that category.

If this is you, ask yourself, "Do I truly like being a softie? Does it secretly irritate me or go against my grain?" If the answer is yes, it's time to alter your reactions to others and perhaps get involved in some social service activities, which will give you a more realistic view of others and help you to build a deeper sense of self-acceptance and confidence.

*"I don't know what it's all about, but we seem to be in on the
ground floor of something or other."*

CHAPTER 2
LOVE AND ROMANCE

YOUR SOCIAL REACTIONS PREDICT YOUR MARITAL HAPPINESS

Predicting marital bliss is a favorite topic of national surveys. The most telling factors in these counts consistently turns out to be the personal traits of the partners, i.e., their maturity, length of engagement, financial security, etc. But there are other earmarks of a happy marriage and they involve our relationships with others. These are the significant people (either past or present) who shape our attitudes and feelings about interpersonal commitment.

Careful research by Lewis Terman of Stanford University confirms that much of the success or failure in the wedded state is connected to our parents, siblings, relatives and friends and knowing the quality of your relationship to them, you can gain an insight into just how your marriage will fare.

The items ahead are drawn from research studies on the subject. Answer True or False to each, then read on.

1. We are (were) close to each of our parents.

2. When young, we both generally showed obedience toward significant adults, i.e. parents, relatives, teachers, etc.

3. Our parents and friends heartily approved of our marriage.

4. When young we were popular and likeable among our peers.

5. Within both of our families combined (sibs, uncles, aunts, etc.) there are fewer than one in 20 divorces or separations.

6. The adults who disciplined us as children, were firm and not lax.

7. We got along well with our intended mother-in-law and father-in-law.

8. We got along with our brothers, sisters or cousins.

EXPLANATION

Of the two million marriages each year, the hard statistics are that about one in three ends in divorce. The rate is even higher in California. When it is compared with approximately one in eight in 1900, it is evident that although marriage can be a supreme joy for many, it also can be a risky venture. Our quiz items indicate that interpersonal relationships reveal telltale signs of how well a marriage will fare. In other words, how a person will react to living intimately with someone is based upon how that person interfaced with many types of people in a variety of situations. Other predictors which forecast compatibility or betoken a future split are:

1. Large age differences between partners (i.e. 12 or 15 years or more).
2. Hasty marriages with less than six months courting.
3. Marriage before the age of 21 years.
4. Working wives who resent having to work.

A finding which crops up over and over again seems to confirm the value of homespun wisdom. It is apparently true that factors which make for a good marriage are strikingly similar to the advice parents traditionally give their children in mate selection. These concern choosing the same social, religious and ethnic background and, in general, finding a mate who has values and a lifestyle similar to one's own family. In general, when two persons consider marriage, the more conventional the relationship, the higher the chance of marriage success.

SCORE

Give yourself a point for each True answer. Consider that the higher your score is above 5, the better is your marital adjustment. The lower your score below 4, the more you'll have to work at your relationship to keep it growing.

For low scorers don't be discouraged. In the last analysis, you can override adverse early influences and still come out ahead of those hard statistics. Your personal maturity and motivation to make a go of it will determine whether yours will be a happy marriage.

ARE YOU A MALE/FEMALE CHAUVINIST PIG?

The battle of the sexes has raged since Eden. Although behavior science rarely goes out on a limb to favor either male or female in this eternal competition, (anthropologist Ashley Montague excepted), there are some factors which definitely distinguish the genders from each other.

While male and female clearly think and behave uniquely about various aspects of living, e.g., work, children, politics, cooking, etc., this is more a reflection of their different environment influences and training rather than of specific instincts.

For example, because of the orientation that our society imposes upon them, women are more concerned with events that involve growth, love, and nurturing, whereas men are more interested in commerce, justice and power. In a nutshell, the way people behave is nearly always governed by environmental influences.

Women's lib brought a spirit of equality between the sexes, yet interesting differences continue to prevail between them that surface repeatedly in surveys.

If you've grown complacent about this unending yet popular topic of party conversation, take the quiz and be prepared for a surprise or two. Answer each item true or false.

1. Women are more suggestible than men. T
2. Men exceed women in verbal fluency and in memory power. T
3. Men tend to be more cheerful and optimistic than women. T
4. The chances of becoming depressed are about the same for both sexes. F
5. Women are more sociable and friendlier than men. T
6. Men smoke more than women do. T
7. Women are more emotional than men. T
8. Women commit suicide more often than men do. F
9. Men are better at math than women are. F
10. Wives understand their husbands better than husbands understand their wives. T

SCORE

1. True. Suggestibility is higher in women, although the differences are small. The main work on this question has been done by hypnosis investigators since suggestibility is almost perfectly correlated with the ability to be hypnotized.

2. False. Women develop verbal skills earlier and retain this edge over men on language ability. On the Wechsler Adult Intelligence Scale, women come out somewhat higher on both verbal and memory ability.

3. True. On personality tests, men as a group tend to show more cheerfulness and optimism than women do.

4. False. Hospitals, psychotherapists and physicians report more depression among women than among men.

5. False. It is a popular misconception that women are more sociable than men but, on the average, men show as much sociability and amicability as women do.

6. True. On the other hand, teenage girls smoke more than adolescent males do, and this trend is increasing annually.

7. True. Probably because of their complex endocrine systems, women show more emotional volatility than men and have a broader range of mood swings as well.

8. False. Men outnumber women in suicides 3-to-1, but women make more attempts at suicide than men do.

9. True. Early in their development, males score higher than females in mathematical reasoning and mechanical aptitude, and they tend to maintain this lead over women.

10. False. Studies by VA psychologist Richard C. Cowden verify husbands show more insight about their wives' personalities than vice versa.

Give yourself 1 point for each correct answer.

8-10 correct: Your understanding of the opposite sex is good.

4-7 correct: You have average insight into your gender counterpart.

0-3 correct: You have more than your share of misconceptions about the opposite sex. More reading on the subject will help

WILL YOU SUCCEED WITH THE OPPOSITE SEX? (WHO WINS THE BATTLE OF THE SEXES?)

Overheard at a cocktail party: He: "This seems to be a man's world alright. Don't you wish you were a man?" She: "Never. Do you?" The debate rages on. Who is superior— man or woman? Ahead are items to test and tease on this universal pastime. Answer each item true or false, then read on.

1. Men daydream about as much as women do.
2. Women fall in love faster than men do.
3. Women have more sex fantasies about men than vice versa.
4. There are no differences in the dreams of men and women.
5. Fathers physically abuse their children more than do mothers.
6. Husbands tend to be more intelligent than their wives.
7. In same-gender friendships, men are more helpful to each other than are women.
8. Men are more honest than women.
9. Men can detect the motives of others better than women can.
10. Women are shier than men.

ANSWERS:

1. True. Professor Jerome Singer of Yale University, an author on the subject, reports: "So far, our studies show very few major differences between the sexes in the pattern and frequency of daydreaming?"

2. False. Brandeis University professor Zick Rubin, whose questionnaires on love have provided a basis for much research, finds that men tend to fall in love faster and fall out of love more slowly than women.

3. False. Alfred Kinsey, the sex researcher, found that men have far more sex fantasies about women than the reverse.

4. False. Dream narratives collected from a large number of men and women show that men dream more about men than they do about women, while women dream equally as often about men and women.

5. False. Several surveys show that mothers abuse their children more often than fathers do. Mothers are the abusive parent in 50 to 80 percent of the cases cited (and mothers kill their children about twice as often as fathers do). One reason may be that a child's actions have more of an adverse impact on the self-esteem and identity of a mother than they do on a father.

6. True. Many studies show that women tend to marry men they can admire intellectually. Men, on the other hand, tend to shun intellectual superiors.

7. False. Research at the University of Utah shows that since they are more self-disclosing, verbal and affectionate, women tend to have more of a therapeutic affect on each other than men have on other men.

8. False. One study of more than 5,000 persons found that women are just as evasive as men, but men are much more capable of telling lies.

9. False. Generally women are more aware of social cues. They show more sensitivity than men in picking up such non-verbal messages as body language, facial expression and tone of voice.

10. False. Shyness is found equally present among men and women. Professor Philip Zimbardo of Stanford University, a leading authority on the subject, found that there is no difference between the genders on shyness.

SCORE:

Give yourself one point for each correct answer.

8 or more points. Your insight into the differences between the sexes is good. You have fewer distortions about them than most people do.

4-7 points. You have an average degree of understanding of men and women.

0-3 points. Chances are you rely too heavily upon stereo-typed notions about the differences between men and women.

WHAT DOES IT TAKE TO MAKE YOU JEALOUS

If you've ever been in a blue funk over the green-eyed monster, you're not alone. Jealousy lies dormant within the darkest reaches of every human heart. It's a fairly normal reaction to actual or imagined loss of affection or gain, from a valued person. It's easy to see that we feel insecure about their esteem or love for us.

Mind-probers have uncovered some hard facts on the subject:

1. It is more common among first-born children than those born later.
2. It is more frequent in smaller families (i.e., two or three children) than in larger ones.
3. And it is more likely between sisters than between brothers.

To gauge how jealous you might be, look at the hypothetical situations ahead. Indicate how disturbed or annoyed you might feel about each occurrence using this scale:

1. Not upset.
2. A little upset.
3. Moderately upset.
4. Very upset.
5. Extremely upset.

If you are single, imagine for the moment, that you have a spouse/partner.

QUIZ

1. An unmarried old flame calls your mate and would like to meet him/her for a drink and some conversation.

2. Your best friend recently became seriously involved with someone and never seems to have as much time to spend with you as before.

3. You and a colleague labored hard on an extremely difficult assignment, however, your boss (or teacher) gave your partner most of the credit.

4. You don't enjoy going to the community center. Your mate, who has a full-time job, spends two weekday evenings and half of Saturday there joining others in activities like swimming, scrabble, book discussions, etc., while you remain home.

5. Your mate and a coworker of the opposite sex are good friends and enjoy occasional lunches together. They provide each other with emotional support on personal matters. Although your partner talks about this person often, you don't know the friend well.

6. At a festive masquerade, you discover your partner in an isolated room, gently kissing another guest he/she met a few hours ago. Later, the explanation you get is: "I had a bit too much to drink. I meant no harm by it."

7. You've tried to reach your partner for over an hour, but the phone line was busy. Later, you're told that the caller was a neighbor, a person who is known to be a "swinger."

8. Your mate calls to say he/she will be working late with an attractive colleague.

9. At a social, your partner, who likes to dance, spends about an hour dancing with an attractive divorced person. You don't dance well and prefer to sit and chat with friends.

10. Your mate hasn't revealed it, but someone tells you that he/she was seen in a cafe with an eye-catching swinger.

EXPLANATION AND SCORING

Jealousy, the unadmitted emotion, is a universal reaction. It begins early in life. Babies as young as six months of age show it when their mothers pay attention to someone else. Children typically show keen disappointment and jealousy when displaced as the only child by a new sibling. This jealousy often continues into childhood as a sibling rivalry and competition with peers. If you're a parent, be on guard lest you unwittingly promote jealousy at home by holding up a child to be a model for others, so soften it a bit.

There is a debate among behaviorists about the origin of jealously. Is it inherited or acquired?

Psychologists E. Aronson and A. Pines of the University of California, Berkeley, believe it is the latter. They developed an extensive 200 item sexual jealousy questionnaire that was administered to several hundred subjects. They found that jealous persons report more overall dissatisfaction with their lives than do others. In addition, they tend to have a lower educational level, more feelings of inferiority and an unflattering self-image.

WHAT YOUR SCORE MEANS

Sum up your score. This is not an official test, of course, but consider that it means the following:

0-20 points. It takes a lot to make you jealous. You're secure in the belief that your partner will be faithful. Be careful; however, don't feel overly confident about human passions in powerful tempting situations.

21-29 points. You have average instincts of jealousy. If the tables were turned in the situations, you'd probably be true to your partner.

30 or more points. Move over Othello. You're the jealous type: Try to understand why this might be so. Do you feel so inferior that you fear easy rejection by others?

ARE WOMEN MORE JEALOUS THAN MEN?

Dr. Robert Bringle of Purdue University, Indiana, recently gave a jealousy test to 1,000 men and women, ages 18 to 48, and discovered that there is no essential difference. The incidence of jealousy is NOT primarily determined by one's gender but rather by the degree of one's self-respect. Those most often and most intensely jealous tend to share low self-esteem and to be distrustful about others. They view the world as combating them and see themselves as losers

WHAT IS YOUR "INTIMACY INDEX"?

Dr. Sidney Jourard of the University of Florida, tells of an elderly man from Maine who, at his 50th wedding anniversary, stood up, placed his hand on his wife's shoulder and said: "Bessie dear, there have been times during the past 50 years when I felt so loving toward you it was all I could do to keep myself from telling you." Sharing personal feeling doesn't come easy for some of us.

Jourard's books, *The Transparent Self* and *Self Disclosure*, summarize interesting facts about how willing we are to share our personal experiences.

If you've ever felt awkward about showing your private feelings, you're not alone. The following quiz may provide a better perspective. Test your knowledge about our subject. Answer true or false to the items. They are based on Jourard's numerous studies.

1. The older one gets, the less the need to disclose personal feelings.

2. Good friendships involve equal self-disclosure between the partners.

3. Friendships between men tend to be just as emotionally revealing as those between women.

4. Usually if you open up to someone, that person will also open up to you.

5. People can still be good friends but not share intimate thoughts and feelings.

6. For most of us, our mother remains the primary person in whom we confide.

7. How much we reveal to a professional (i.e., doctor, clergyman, etc.) doesn't have much to do with how much we personally like him or her.

8. Married folks have less need to reveal themselves to others than do singles.

9. If we don't naturally divulge ourselves to others it is a sign that we are strong enough to solve our own problems.

10. Men and women are about equal in their occasional use of friendship as a sounding board for frustration.

EXPLANATION

1. False. Analyzing over 1000 subjects, Jourard found that as we grow older, we become more willing to reveal ourselves. An older person, it seems, is less defensive and more open to ties, which will enrich his/her life.

2. False. We can't expect a perfect 50/50 match. Many good couples are not equally balanced because one partner may have more need for intimacy than the other, yet the friendship (or marriage) may thrive for years.

3. False. A study by Robert Bell of Temple University reported that friendships between women are more personal and emotionally based than those between men.

4. True. During his 12 years of research, Jourard, the foremost authority on self-disclosure, consistently found that when we open up to someone, he/she tends to respond in kind.

5. False. It can't be validly said that there is a friendship unless intimate feelings are shared. There is often confusion about being an acquaintance and being a friend. The latter means being emotionally involved to some degree.

6. True. For both sexes, it is true that mother, more than father or close peers, is our confidant, but only until the time of marriage. From then on, we confide more in our spouse than anyone else, although mother remains our second choice.

7. False. It's natural to confide in a professional, however, studies show that our self-disclosures increase in proportion to how much we like the person we consult.

8. False. Marriage doesn't alter our need to communicate. Marrieds reveal as much as singles do, but their audience is narrower. They open up more to their spouse than to others.

9. False. The opposite is more likely. When we are reticent or unwilling to expose our self we tend to be fragile emotionally. There is a connection between reticence to self-disclose and emotional maladjustment.

10. False. Independent research by professors Helen Hacker of Adelphi University and Sherwin Davidson of the University of Utah confirms that not only are women more self-revealing than men, they approach friendships as a form of "therapy" more so than do men.

SCORE

Take a point for each correct answer. If you have 7-8 points, your understanding of self-disclosure is high, 4-6 points, you are average on this factor, and if you have 3 or fewer points, your understanding of self-disclosure is low.

Note: Opening up to others is largely a matter of balancing the potential rewards of intimacy against the possible risk of rejection or betrayal. For the sake of your mental health, an intimate catharsis is often beneficial. It's better to open up to one you trust than keep troubling feelings bottled inside.

DO YOU GET TRAPPED IN SUNSHINE?
(ARE YOU A GOOD A JUDGE OF OTHERS?)

We all "goof" once in a while when it comes to sizing up others. Many errors are due to false assumptions we absorb in the form of folklore, myth and rumors. In turn, these false views often cause conflicts.

The number of faulty notions a society harbors depends upon its historical traditions. Studies confirm that older cultures are more steeped in imperfect and archaic views of people. Psychological research conducted in modern societies, on the other hand, has brought considerable insight and a more accurate perception of human nature.

The following quiz offers you a chance to face your untested assumptions about behavior. Mark true or false to each item.

1. We become sadder as we grow older.
2. You can judge someone's personality from a photograph.
3. Fast learners forget more than slow learners.
4. There's a thin line between genius and insanity.
5. In a happy marriage, compared with those which are unhappy, partners have sex more frequently.
6. Venting anger at someone reduces its physical and emotional ill effects on us.
7. Handwriting can reveal one's personality.
8. Unhappy people live just as long as happy people.
9. Men smoke more than women do.
10. Women in business tend to be more emotional than men.

EXPLANATION

All items are false.

1. We don't become sad because of age. A national survey by the National Council on Aging in Washington D.C. showed that less than one-fourth of those over 65 report, "This is the dreariest time of my life," while a majority said, "I am just as happy as when I was younger."

2. Many studies fail to show that personality traits, as well as mental ability, can be judged from photos. Video pictures don't increase the accuracy of those judgments appreciably either.

3. Fast learners usually have higher intelligence and they tend to remember more of what they learn than their slow-learner counterparts.

4. The genius has often be thought to be" different", i.e., mad, unsocial, sickly, etc. This notion has no foundation in fact. One long-term study of over 1300 gifted children by the late professor Lewis Terman of Stanford University, showed that they grew up superior in many ways: i.e., better health, better social adjustment, higher grades, etc., and when older, landed better jobs.

5. How often couples have sex has more to do with their emotional makeup than their happiness. Some happy couples are content with less sex compared with those who are unhappy. The important thing is whether both partners are satisfied with the frequency of their lovemaking.

6. This is a common misunderstanding about anger that isn't always true. Recent investigations by Dr. Leonard Berkowitz of the University of Wisconsin at Madison, showed that in the process of telling someone off we frequently stimulate ourselves to continued or even stronger aggression.

7. There is no scientific proof that one's personality can be analyzed through script. This has been called a "gold brick" psychology because its claims are louder than the hard facts.

8. Dr. Erdman Palmore of Duke University, devised a "longevity index" to predict the life span of people over 65. Using several hundred subjects he found that those who rated themselves as happy tended to live longer. His index proved to be more accurate than the actuarial tables of insurance companies.

9. Both genders smoke to about the same degree, however, girls exceed boys in smoking.

10. This cliché abounds throughout the world. The facts show that women managers display no more emotion or drama about their work than men do.

SCORE

Take a point for each correct answer. A score of 6 or 7 shows an average degree of insight into behavior and personality. If you scored 4 or less, we suggest a good book or a course in human behavior. Chances are it will improve your relationships with others and lead the way to greater self-knowledge.

ARE YOU HARD-HEARTED?

You join a crowd gathered around a painter who fell from a ladder. A man next to you looks down at the injured workman and remarks: "It's been a bad day for Stan Adams.".You ask, "Is that the poor guy who's lying there?" "No", the bystander replies, "I'm Stan Adams"

As far as the capacity to be aware of what someone else is feeling, then Stan Adams certainly would fail the quiz ahead and rate zero on social sensitivity. Our story is unlikely, for practically everyone has some degree of this trait. Without this quality of compassion, it would be impossible to relate to others even in the most primitive way. It's necessary for meaningful relationships.

Professors Jonathan Cheek of Wellesley College, John Johnson of Penn. State University and Robert Smither of Georgetown University did extensive study on empathy. Their findings confirm that those low on this trait wind up having difficulty with others.

If your social life isn't as good as it should be, it might mean an empathy deficit. The items ahead could reveal the answer. They are adapted from those used by the researchers above.

Answer the items: Rarely 1 point, Sometimes, 2 points, Often 3 points.

1. I take an active part in the entertainment at parties.
2. I show a talent for influencing the ideas of others.
3. I care about what others think of me.
4. I enjoy romantic novels more than political non-fiction.
5. I have seen things so sad that I almost felt like crying.
6. I have more patience with people than most of my friends do.
7. I exceed the speed limit when I drive.
8. Under no circumstances would I buy an item I suspected was stolen.

For items 9 and 10, answer: 1 True, 2 Partly True, 3 Not True.

9. I am cross or grumpy without any good reason.

10. I think the country would be better off if we had some drastic changes in government.

EXPLANATION

Social harmony demands a willingness to respect another person's state of mind or emotions. It's a central necessity in all human affairs. We learn to resonate with the inner experiences of others from an early age. Infants, barely 2 months old, have been observed to smile when others smile. By 9 or 10 months, they will cry, babble and rock copying what other babies are doing. This mirroring of acts and gestures marks the early start of identification, which later progresses to empathy for the feelings, actions and beliefs of others.

Empathy is related to a number of personality traits such as self-confidence (items 1 & 2), sensitivity to others (3, 4 & 5), even-temperedness (6 & 7). and respect for others (8 & 9).

A somewhat unusual connection also exists with another personal characteristic. Those with radical or anti-establishment attitudes (non-conformity and refractory ideas) tend to have low empathy (items 9 & 10).

ARE YOU TOO DISTRUSTFUL TO FALL IN LOVE?

Like it or not, as members of human society, our trust in others is a condition for survival. Even in so simple an act as eating a cookie, we trust that it hasn't been tampered with.

The bottom line is that enjoying the benefits of societal living requires that we build a trusting dependence upon one another. And, in our impersonal world, being trusted may well represent a greater compliment than being loved.

By the time we are adults, we've learned whether or not to trust others, based on our own experiences and not totally on the views of others. But sometimes we go overboard. For example, a grocer who once received a bad check for $139 vowed that it would never happen again. As a result, he refused checks for six years, even when the checks came from his best customers. Unfortunately, he had succumbed to an all too human tendency, 'response generalization'. That is, he applied the lessons of a bad experience to everyone he encountered.

Trusting someone also depends upon the setting. You might trust a stranger you meet at a church function more than you would trust a stranger in a cocktail lounge.

Trusting someone depends on judgment as well. You might trust a friend to feed your pet in your absence but would not trust the same friend to keep a secret. Yet trusting isn't completely reliant on setting or judgment. There is a general personality trait that has been identified as 'interpersonal trust'.

Psychologists C. Johnson-George and W. Swap of Tufts University, in Medford, Mass, have done extensive investigation in this area, and have found that on questionnaires females make more trusting ratings than do males.

But these findings need not suggest that people can be conclusively categorized as trusting or untrusting by gender alone. If you are wondering what your 'trust index' is compared to others, the following quiz may provide some insight. The quiz is based on research done at Tufts. Answer each item true or false, then read on for explanations.

1. I am reluctant to lend money to others because of the hassle involved in getting it back.

2. Most people who compliment others are only flattering them and don't really mean what they say.

3. Most people would intentionally misrepresent their point of view if it benefited them.

4. Most people who borrow something and return it slightly damaged probably wouldn't mention it to their lender.

5. Most people today are too dependent on others.

6. I can take people or leave them

7. If a company told its employees that profits were too low to grant pay raises, I would tend to be suspicious of the firm's honesty.

8. Most politicians have taken bribes.

9. Most successful people get ahead because of who they know rather than what they know.

10. People today have lower moral standards than people did a generation ago.

ANSWERS

Give yourself 1 point for each false answer.

8-10 correct. You are a trusting person who accepts others as you see them. You may have a tendency to be so accepting of others that you might even be gullible or naive.

5-7 correct. You have a balance between trust and caution. You're open to new relationships but can maintain a fair amount of objectivity when it comes to trusting others.

0-4 correct. You are more guarded and suspicious than most people. You probably analyze others' motives too much. Your trouble, like the grocer, will be in lowering your suspicions when dealing with honest people.

Interpersonal trust involves risk. The question will always be: Will the gain outweigh the chance of betrayal or rejection?

Dr. Carl Rogers, founder of the humanist movement in psychology and former director of the Center for the Study of the Human Person in La Jolla, California concluded after much research that realistic trust and acceptance of others usually go along with self-acceptance and are indicators of a well-adjusted personality.

CAN YOU SPOT A FLIRT?

Involvement is a goal of most humans. But in a busy impersonal world, it's a challenge which occurs on many levels and flirting is one of them. Because of its unflattering connotation, maybe it would be better not to call it flirting but signaling, if you will. It is learned behavior and there is evidence that a signaling system exists which is universally understood and occurs through our body movements.

If you watch TV ads, you'll be assailed with the sport. Savvy advertisers likely will admit that those femmes fatales or virile men who extol the virtues of soap, soda and SUVs are flirting with you. Look for the stare, the eye blink, the hair toss, etc. This makes otherwise boring ads interesting.

Although studies on it are rare, flirting behavior is a bona fide form of social communication with a goal. When Mae West teased "come up and see me sometime" she and everyone else were delightfully aware of her intent. Although frowned on by society, the world's oldest art is done either subtly or openly. Often this overture to interaction is non-verbal, semi-conscious and basically a friendly gesture.

Most of us hesitate to approach strangers without a friendly sign of interest from them. Instead, we might begin a series of unwitting, though conspicuous body movements, which reveal that a signaling is in progress.

Can you spot it when someone (or even you) is flirting?

Pretend you are watching a couple conversing. Check off any items below (and here are only a few), which might tell that flirting is in progress:

1. fingering, smoothing or rearranging one's hair
2. adjusting clothing, i.e., sock straightening
3. opening or closing buttons, zippers etc.
4. wiping or adjusting eyeglasses
5. doodling with jewelry
6. chin stroking
7. excessive smiling, giggling or laughing
8. moving facial parts
9. raising or lowering eyebrows
10. lip pouting
11. waving hands or arms
12. leaning forward
13. touching
14. finger tapping
15. hugging
16. cheek kissing
17. ear tugging
18. scratching
19. extending fingers, hands, arms, legs, or feet
20. flexing muscles
21. body stretching
22. body self -stroking

23. staring
24. gazing (lowering or aversion)
25. winking
26. strong steady eye contact.

Our list can be grouped as follows:

Preening (items 1-7). Here we display interest in someone by movements which make us more attractive to them.

Posture Synchrony (item 8-12). Kinesiologists find that when two persons are mutually attracted, they tend to mirror each other's bodily movements and stances.

Touching (items 13-16). Body contact is often a flirting gesture. It could be as simple as a tap on the arm or shoulder to a hug or kiss on the cheek and it is usually non-sexual. The one who initiates the touching (most often the man) is the more dominant one.

Automanipulation (items 17-22). These movements draw attention to ourselves.

Eye movements (items 23-26). Eye behavior is most significant. When eye contact is made, it's a solid signal of mutual interest.

EXPLANATION

Kinesics, the study of body movements, began with the work of anthropologist Raymond Birdwhistell at the University of California. When we flirt, we send signals which say, "I am not threatening, and I'm open to being friendly. Will you be interested in me?"

It was Dr. Albert Scheflen, formerly of Albert Einstein College of Medicine, NY and author of *Body Movement and Social Order*, who established kinesics as a science. He found that body movements control and maintain social order and they appear in behavior patterns as diverse as greeting, courting and negotiation.

Let's be quick to add, for naysayers who would condemn it, flirting, like most of man's inventions, can be used for good or mischief. It's an invitation of sorts, a necessary prologue for species survival but it gives the target a chance to demur and, happily, allows both parties to retreat and save face. If, however, the target responds with availability signals, then the ensuing relationship may range from slight acquaintance to sexual escapade to marriage.

But it isn't a simple matter. Studies by sociologist Dr. Mark Gary of Temple University, Philadelphia, show that if a woman doesn't return eye contact, most men will not pursue her. And thereby hangs a moral, to wit: Flirting is for one who gambles; be prepared for gain or shambles.

SCORE

A mature adult should get at least 15 "hits" on this quiz.

IS YOUR LOVE REAL OR JUST INFATUATION?

Love is a weightless imponderable like electricity or magnetism. No on has ever explained it yet everyone needs it. Whether young or old, meek or mighty we all seek the secure feeling that we are valued by someone. But humans possess an unhappy capacity, the stronger the need for something, the more they fool themselves about it.

Scientists have given the problem of love vs. infatuation some thought and the conclusions may help you decide if it's the real thing.

The quiz items are drawn from actual research studies. Answer yes or no to each. Try to be as honest as you can.

1. Do you catch yourself daydreaming a good deal about your partner?
2. Did you fall in love within a very short time, (say less than 7 or 8 dates)?
3. Do you tend to fall in and out of love easily?
4. Are you frequently surprised at the notions or behavior of your partner?
5. Do you notice that you both brag a bit too much to friends about each other?
6. Do you often reassure each other verbally that your love is real?
7. Do you find it easy to overlook your partner's faults?
8. Is sexual attraction a dominant factor in your involvement?
9. In your romance, is the man strong and dominant and the woman very coy and passive?
10. Do you tell friends about the intimacies you share with your partner?

EXPLANATION

The items are drawn from actual questionnaires used in research. The most prominent is that of Dr. Zick Rubin of Harvard University. His reports in the *Journal of Personality and Social Psychology* are recognized throughout the world.

1. The daydreams of infatuated persons center on themselves and how much pleasure their beloved will bring them. Mature love focuses on the other person. Your plans and interests should keep organizing themselves around your partner and to a lesser degree, around yourself.

2. Love at first sight means you've fallen for an idealized lover, one you've created and kept alive in your fantasy. Although he or she might resemble your mental image in looks, actions or beliefs, you tend to exaggerate feelings of familiarity toward him or her because you've already "known" him or her in the privacy of your own thoughts for a time

3. If you fall in and out of love easily it's probably because your needs for love are very strong and you're quick to latch on to anyone who is close to what you're seeing. Chances are you've been working overtime on that idealized image of a partner.

4. Look for these subtle clues of infatuation. If you keep being surprised by your partner, chances are you really haven't judged him/her accurately and don't really know them as well as you believe.

5. Romantic love usually has plenty of mutual exploitation in it. When we brag, we boost our own ego rather than satisfy the desires of our partner.

6. Couples who spend a good deal of time reassuring each other of their devotion are probably protesting too much. Their constantly reasserted love usually betrays plenty of inner doubt they have about each other.

7. Blocking out of our partner's faults is the defense of denial. It might be covering something too painful to admit. A mature lover sees and accepts faults in his beloved and has a good confidence that he can deal with them.

8. Children are attracted to external appearances rather than true qualities in their world. Some of us never outgrow this tendency to judge others by their looks. The mature lover has learned the truth of the statement that the most important things about people are invisible.

9. Male dominance and female passivity are exaggerated romantic roles which were portrayed in medieval stories when love took the form of coquetry, lyrical poems and tales. In this day and age, this is almost certain to be an immature match.

10. Mature love dislikes revealing intimacies to outsiders We might feel there is a bit of prestige to be gained in it but sharing our privacy with others is like giving it away and love abhors losing any of its totality. It wants to keep, hold and cherish.

SCORE

All items are correctly marked No. Take one point for every No answer.

A score of 8 or more, you seem to be making a mature choice. Between 5 and 7, you have a few blind spots to clear up before your match will succeed well. 4 or less, think twice about your decision. You've been hit with a starry-eyed myopia which is likely to burst your bubble of romance.

"She's in the bathtub with Mr. Jenkins right now."

CHAPTER 3
HOME AND FAMILY

ARE YOU A FAMILY MENACE? (DO YOU PRACTICE GOOD SAFETY HABITS?)
After skidding into a tree, a shaken motorist was asked by a policeman: "Why were you speeding?" The dazed driver replied in serious tones: "My fuel supply was low and I figured I'd better rush to the service station before my gas ran out." This story may not be worth a chuckle, but accidents to the National Safety Council in Chicago are no joke. They report that over 7 million Americans suffered disabling accidents and some 29,000 deaths in the year 2006. Most of these occurred not on the highway, as might be believed, but in the home. This supposed sanctuary of safety leads all other locations (i.e., work, school, roads, etc.), in mishaps by 3 to 1, indeed home is where the hurt is. A fatal injury happens here every 18 minutes and a disabling one, every 4 seconds. The top 4 causes are: poisoning, fires and burns, suffocation, and falls. The American Academy of Orthopedic Surgeons tell us that falls are a leading cause of injuries to seniors, with 11 million falls in 2001. That's 1 out of every 3 for those over 65 years of age.

Are you a help or a hazard around the house? Do accidents seem to hit you more than others? The quiz gives you a chance to study yourself.

Answer True or False to the items. Be honest.

I have:
1. Dropped razor blades into the wastebasket.
2. Continued to use electric appliances which have a worn cord.
3. Moved an electric fan without disconnecting it.
4. Used a dull knife which required strong pressure to make it cut.
5. Touched electrified objects like hair dryer, shaver, light switch, etc., with moist hands.
6. Kept oily rags or furniture polish cloths in non-metal containers like plastic bags, cardboard boxes, etc.
7. Placed a scatter rug at the top or bottom of a stairway.
8. Stored an electric appliance by first removing the cord from the appliance and then disconnecting the cord from the wall outlet.
9. Used a fork or knife to dislodge toaster bread.
10. Put knives in the drawer with points toward me.

11. Driven without a seat belt, or drank or eaten while driving.

12. Left knives out on the counter top with kids around.

13. Stored wax paper, foil wrap, cling wrap boxes with cutting edges up.

14. Have not had Radon testing done on my home.

15. Left stovetop burners on after cooking.

16. Left toddlers or infants alone with our family pet.

17. Not taught my kids never to tease our pet.

18. Drunk a hot liquid with a child in my lap.

19. Not kept balloons, button-cell batteries, toys, nuts, etc. away from infants.

20. Not worn gloves when using heavy tools

EXPLANATION

Pulling a safety boner is largely a matter of poor judgment and personality make-up. A small percentage of people, 25 % or so, have the majority of accidents. Those in this accident-prone group falsely believe they will be spared. But grim statistics show their folly. Their mishap rate is 5 to 1 compared with others. They have personality traits all their own. First, they are victimized by the myth of personal exclusion (it only happens to the other guy—it won't happen to me). They tend to be in the 15-24 year old range and are usually impulsive, maladjusted and thrill seekers.

Psychoanalysts say they may even have self-directed hostility. But other less fancy reasons are: excessive worry, inattentiveness, non-concern for self, poor perceptual problems, poor muscle sense, etc.

Fatigue also plays a role here. At work, for example, 50% of all accidents happen in the last 2 hours of the day compared with 20% in the first 2 hours.

SCORE

Take one point for each true answer.

0-4 points. You are keenly safety conscious.

5-9 points. You're in the average range. But you should shoot for even more awareness about possible hazards around you

10-15 points. You're unconscious of your surroundings and accident traps in day-to-day living. Look around and ask: What can I do to prevent a possible mishap?

TIPS ON SAFETY

Since fatigue is an important cause of accidents, don't attempt tasks which require alertness for example when you're tired and using a ladder, working with sharp or power tools, taking that extra swim, or another run on the ski slope. Never be complacent about your surroundings. Make a quick survey to spot its potential dangers, and then take action to correct these to keep you and your family safe. Remember, safety is no accident

WHEN TEMPERS FLARE COULD YOUR FAMILY BECOME VIOLENT?

A current news story tells of a father who killed his family then committed suicide. We may think of home as society's last bastion of security, but not only is this false, its opposite is more likely. Violence, like charity, begins at home. It includes child abuse, wife beating, rape and incest and most of these incidents are reported with reluctance, if at all.

Since it is often suppressed, it is hard to estimate how often such violence occurs. In 1990 the American Humane Association, reported that child protective services documented about 820,000 cases of child abuse. By 1996, the figure increased 22% to about 1 million.

In every state, it is legal for a parent to strike a child. Indeed, it is only parents and police who have a clear mandate to use force to alter behavior. Such laws hardly need publicity. It would be difficult to find an American "institution" more consistently violent than the family unit. Possibly because of the emotion surrounding the issue, many false notions arise about home violence. One popular myth is that a husband is the primary aggressor and his wife, the passive recipient of his wrath. But there is now plenty of evidence to dispel this myth. Husbands are also battered by their wives. Do you have false notions about America's spiraling shame? The quiz ahead will tell. Answer each item True or False, then read on.

1. Most child abuse cases reported involve members of low-income families.

2. Most domestic disputes center on sex, love and affection.

3. While injuries occur frequently in family battles, fewer than 10 % of all homicides occur at home.

4. Because they have fewer family members to focus on, parents of small families hit their children more than parents of larger families.

5. When a couple fights, a wife is more likely than her husband is to be a homicide victim.

6. Peer pressure is the main cause of the increase in the number of children who commit aggressive acts against their own loved ones.

7. In almost all cases, the assailant starts the fight that leads to his victim's death.

8. Overall, husbands file as many domestic violence complaints including child abuse, spouse beating, etc., as do their wives.

9. Most child abuse victims are above the age of 5.

10. When police disrupt a family quarrel, their presence is usually enough to calm down its members.

EXPLANATION

1. True. Child abuse cases involving low-income families surface more often, but the rate reflects a reporting bias. Clinics and social agencies rarely deal with affluent families. Furthermore, police, doctors and therapists are hesitant to report clashes in affluent families; nonetheless, many experts believe that, like alcoholism, family strife is a problem that plagues all social classes and economic levels.

2. False. The main irritant in family quarrels is over money. A study done by the department of sociology at Portland State University, Oregon revealed that a husband's inadequate income was the source of 84% of serious conflicts.

3. False. Approximately 2000 homicides per year occur within the primary group. This represents about 25% of all homicides nationwide.

4. False. Parents with many children use physical punishment more often than parents with small families.

5. False. A husband is just as likely to be killed by his spouse. But more women than men commit suicide after the deed.

6. False. The cause of increased household disturbance by children is usually in-house stress and, when children act out at home, the violence is usually impulsive.

7. False. Criminologist Marvin Wolfgang of the University of Pennsylvania found that in as many as 1 out of 4 homicide cases the victim was first to use force.

8. False. Wives file family abuse complaints twice as often as do husbands. When husbands are battered, they rarely report it out of embarrassment.

9. False. Children are most vulnerable to harm between the ages of 3 months and 3 years.

10. True. Although it's true that police on the scene usually restore order, at the same time, they face unexpected danger. About 20% of officers killed in the line of duty die while breaking up a family fight. Often the officer is perceived by the aggressor as an ally of the opposing family member.

SCORE
Consider that a score of 6 or more correct answers shows that you have a good grasp of the true factors which cause family violence.

Note: The topic of violence among intimates seems neglected by social scientists. Perusal of the index for the Journal of Marriage and the Family for 30 years (1939-1969) showed not a single article which contained the word "violence" in the title indicating a possible research taboo even among professionals on the subject.

CAN YOU SPOT AN UNHAPPY MARRIAGE, EVEN IF IT'S YOUR OWN?
Taking the notion that forewarned is forearmed; psychologists have probed the factors that foretell interpersonal compatibility and those that signal a future split. Thousands of single and married people have answered elaborate, lengthy questionnaires designed to predict chances of success in their marriage and several studies reveal significant clues that could signal a bumpy road ahead for a couple.

One such study was done by Professor Graham. B. Spanier of the State University of Pennsylvania. He found that seemingly insignificant activities like penny-pinching and showing affection were relevant factors that can determine marital bliss or misery.

The following quiz is based on Spanier's findings. To estimate yours (or someone else's) marriage happiness, answer "yes" or "no" to each item then read on for explanations.

QUIZ

1. The partners have many friends in common.
2. Either partner often leaves the house after an argument.
3. They often criticize each other in front of friends.
4. They usually drift apart at a party, not meeting until it's over.
5. They often laugh together.
6. They spend most of their free time together.
7. They show much mutual affection, i.e., touching, hugging, kissing.
8. They have similar ideas about budgeting money.
9. They often argue heatedly in front of others.
10. They have temporarily separated 2 or more times.

EXPLANATION

While there are no "right" or "wrong" answers, the following responses reflect those given most often by happily wedded couples.

1. Yes. Friends who are mutually enjoyed and are a source of satisfaction tend to strengthen a partnership and keep it going.

2. No. Research indicates that leaving home is far from the best way to handle a spat. In fact, Spanier found that this type of "retreat behavior" is a sign of a shaky relationship.

3. No. Ribbing is a game couples often play with each other. But when it's done with a straight face and especially if the same put-downs are repeated frequently, chances are the union is shaky.

4. No. Even if they drift apart at a social, happy couples tend to meet occasionally, (even if briefly) through the course of an evening. There is an unseen unity between them that endures even when separated.

5. Yes. Sharing laughs is a strong sign of contentment. Those who don't share humor or good feeling often don't enjoy their relationship.

6. Yes. The desire to spend time together is a telling clue to whether a couple is in love. When spouses prefer isolation or solitary events vs. dual activities, it's a sign of trouble.

7. Yes. Open expressions of love that are spontaneous and genuine are the best single sign of a solid union. Ultimately, this also means sexual contentment as well.

8. Yes. Agreement about money matters is crucial to a good match. The facts show that, contrary to what TV soaps tell us, it's not sexual infidelity that disrupts marriages as much as fights about money.

9. No. Arguing often is not a good signal and arguing with" heat" in front of others shows lack of control and a public put down of one's partner.

10. No. Spanier found that splits, even brief ones, accustom people to the more serious decision to divorce. Here the unsolved problems only incubate and probably intensify.

Spanier did an extensive survey of all research done on the topic in the past 20 years, and other interesting findings emerged. For example, though dual-career marriages require special adjustments, a wife's career doesn't adversely hurt a union, even when there are children. If she enjoys her job and he doesn't object to her working outside of the home, having a two-career household needn't be a downer.

Marital adjustment is also influenced significantly by the kind of marriage our parents had. Children of divorced parents are themselves more likely to divorce. It's important to stress here that they do not necessarily inherit a disposition for a" bad" union, they simply adopt the attitude that divorce is an acceptable solution to a tough situation. So this group may need to try a little harder to make their marriage work out.

In general, the more similar the individuals' backgrounds are, the more likely they'll enjoy a happy marriage. However, there are many blissful unions in which partners are of different social, racial and religious backgrounds. Much depends on the willingness of both spouses to make it all work.

SCORE
Take 1 point for each correct answer. Consider that a score of 8 or more shows a good marital adjustment. Scores between 5 and 7 show average adjustment and scores less than 4 show that the union needs repair.

HOW DIFFERENT ARE BOYS AND GIRLS ?
We love our children dearly and to each we give equal concern, but it would be a mistake to regard boys and girls as having the same personality traits. To do so often leads to their rebellion and resentment.

To test your knowledge of the differences between boys and girls answer true or false to the items ahead. They are drawn from studies at leading universities and child-care centers throughout the world.

COMPARING BOYS AND GIRLS:
1. Girls are more social than boys.
2. In infancy, boys are more prone to illness.
3. Girls are just as aggressive as boys.
4. Girls are generally kinder to others.
5. Girls develop more emotional problems.
6. Family stress has a greater impact on girls.
7. Boys are more vulnerable to psychological hang-ups.
8. Girls are just as likely to become delinquents.
9. On tests, boys work faster than girls.
10. Generally, boys are better at math than girls are.

ANSWERS:

1. True. Girls tend to learn social skills earlier than boys; hence they show sociability traits at an earlier age.

2. True. Boys are more vulnerable to prenatal and birth defects. They are somewhat more likely to die as infants and are miscarried more often. They also are more prone to develop childhood diseases.

3. False. Starting between the ages of 2 and 3, boys are more likely to engage in roughhouse than girls. This pattern continues throughout life and holds up through almost every culture in the world.

4. False. Research by Eleanor Maccoby of Stanford University finds no evidence that girls are kinder. Her work shows that both genders are capable of strong altruistic reactions, even as young as 1 or 2 years of age.

5. False. Girls tend to report fears more often than boys do, usually because boys are conditioned to believe it's manly to hold feelings in. As adults, however, women show more depression and phobias than men.

6. False. Several studies show that boys are more vulnerable to tensions in the family. They tend to suffer more intensely and for longer periods of time. Some experts believe this is so because boys get less support from their peers, parents and teachers when the going gets tough.

7. True. Boys tend to be more vulnerable to psychological problems than girls. One survey showed that during first grade boys are referred for psychological help about 10 times as often as girls are. Most of these problems are about aggressive behavior.

8. False. For generations, boys led girls in delinquency by a ratio of 5 to 1. Today, however, this has changed very much. Because of more independence in behavior and attitudes, girls are more assertive in their actions. Though boys are still responsible for most acts of delinquency, arrests of girls are on the rise. The ratio is now about 3 to 1.

9. False. In a study involving more than 8,000 males and females ranging in age from 2 to 90 from across the United States, Vanderbilt University researchers Stephen Camarata and Richard Woodcock discovered that females have a significant advantage over males on timed tests and tasks. Camarata and Woodcock found the differences were particularly significant among pre-teens and teens.

10. False. Janet Hyde, (University of Wisconsin), whose research is reported in the journal *Science* says that, contrary to long-held stereotypes, girls are proving that they are just as capable as boys when it comes to math. In the largest study of its kind, she found that girls measured up to boys in every class, from second through 11th. grades.

SCORE:

Give yourself 1 point for each correct answer. A score of 6 or more can be considered above average.

SHOULD KIDS BE SPANKED?

Do you believe disobedient kids should be flogged? Physical punishment of children is a controversy which predictably resurfaces every few years. In a landmark decision, the U.S. Supreme Court (*Baker vs. Owens*, 1976), ruled that spanking is permissible when: (1) lesser punishment has failed; (2) a student ignores warnings that he will be spanked; (3) a second school official is called to hear the pupil's protests; and (4) the same official is witness to the spanking.

Family specialist and sociologist William J. Goode of Stanford University has done considerable research on child-parent relationships. One large study of his, supported by a grant from the National Science Foundation and written up in the *Journal of Marriage and the Family*, revealed a number of interesting facts about corporal punishment and its effects on the actions of children. One conclusion is that attitudes about punishment can have long-range effects upon children's behavior.

The quiz ahead is based upon Goode's findings. Mark each item true or false, then read on to learn how much you know about the subject of physical discipline.

1. Lower-class parents are more likely to punish their kids physically than middle and upper class parents.

2. Even if one parent tends to be somewhat lax in discipline, a kid is less likely to be aggressive if the other parent is strict.

3. Youngsters in large families tend to escape chastisement for aggressiveness more than those in small families.

4. A teenage boy is less likely to become an alcoholic if he receives consistent control and punishment from his father.

5. The number of brothers and sisters in a family does not appreciably affect how a father disciplines his sons.

6. The more parents perceive God as a punishing being, the more they will tend to punish their kids.

7. More than likely, homosexual males, as youths, were treated in a lax and permissive fashion by their mothers.

8. Parents who have much marital conflict tend to be more lenient with their children.

EXPLANATION

1. True. There is more reliance upon bodily punishment in lower class than in either middle or upper class families. Parents from the latter classes tend to use psychological rather than physical punishment.

2. False. It does not "balance" a family to have parents at opposite ends of a discipline scale. There is actually more of a chance that kids will be aggressive if this is the case rather than if both parents are too lax or too strict.

3. False. Studies show that the larger the family the more the tendency to use physical punishment in socializing the kids.

4. False. The more controlling and punitive a father is over a son, the more likely the son will resort to drinking. This type of discipline is also associated with other anti-social acts such as lying, stealing or truancy.

5. False. The number of sons in a family does tend to influence parents in the disciplining process. For example, fathers are more likely to use physical punishment on boys if all their siblings are brothers than they are on the boy whose siblings are sisters.

6. True. Parents who fear the wrath of God for their transgressions will tend to carry this attitude over toward their offspring. To quote Goode: "The severity of parental punishment for disobedience is paralleled by a belief in supernatural punishment from disobedience to the gods".

7. False. Many homosexuals have had a disturbed tie with either mother, father or both parents. Compared to other mothers, it is likely that the mother of a homosexual is harder on her son in matters of discipline and doles out more whippings to him.

8. False. The more marital friction there is the more parents will adopt physical punishment as the principal means of modifying the behavior of their kids.

SCORE

Your score indicates your understanding of physical discipline, what instigates it and how it affects the reactions of children. Take 1 point for each right answer.

6-8 points. Above average.

3-5 points. Average.

0-2 points. Below average

Much of the fervor for bringing corporal punishment back as a curb against disobedience is a reaction against the teachings of men like Sigmund Freud, Benjamin Spock and John Dewey and the permissiveness of the 1930's and 1940's. But although a growing number of educators approve of physical punishment, the fact is that the vast majority of them do not.

Note: Should it be the case that you're using increasingly excessive measures to correct your child's behavior patterns, it's likely that you need to change your approach. It might be wise to see a child specialist about the matter.

ARE YOU A CONCERNED MOTHER?

Being a mother, a good mother, is probably the world's most difficult challenge. With the pace of life moving at such high speed, it often happens that kids are not only expected to be obedient but to be on their own in many day-to-day tasks of living.

Do you, mother, become so caught up with responsibilities that you overlook the needs of your kids?

Our test may help you be a better Mom and to detect what your child requires to grow up feeling loved and wanted.

Answer the items true or false. They are drawn from lengthy questionnaires by researchers in the field of psychology.

1. I make it a special occasion to reward my children when they get straight A's on their report card.

2. I often excuse myself when my child wants to play with me.

3. I attend a sufficient number of meetings in which my child is involved, i.e., PTA, scouts, school events.

4. I praise my child in front of others.

5. I criticize my child in front of others.

6. I usually admit it when I'm wrong.

7. I hug, touch or kiss my children even though they may be in their early teens.

8. I spend some time explaining to my children what I do in work for my church, community, club, etc.

EXPLANATION

1. TRUE Just as you would like recognition for any job you've done well, so too your child would enjoy special praise for any accomplishments.

2. FALSE To a child, play is communication. More often than not, you shouldn't pass up the chance to play with your child.

3. TRUE You will understand your child better if you are involved in the activities which take up their time and efforts.

4. TRUE Perks done before others is always a good idea (provided it isn't embarrassing to your child, however).

5. FALSE It's not a good idea to parade their errors publicly. It's best and more constructive to criticize privately.

6. TRUE If you want your child to grow to be mature enough to admit mistakes then give him/her a role model to follow and admit your own.

7. TRUE Physical contact serves many basic security needs and, we never outgrow our need for it.

8. TRUE It will help your children to know you better if you give them some idea of what you do when away from home.

SCORE

All answers should be marked True except 2 & 5. The higher your score above 5, the higher you rate as a mother.

Question: What is worse, bad fathering or bad mothering?

Research in Australia by Wayne Warburton, at Macquarie University's Children and Families Research Centre, provides evidence that bad mothering has a worse effect on children than bad fathering. Mothers who exhibit "toxic" behaviors, from being cold and indifferent to being abusive, manipulative or over-controlling, are far more likely to warp their children's outlook on life than fathers with similar behavior.

ARE YOU A CONCERNED FATHER?

In our satiric society everything comes up for its shot on the Lampoon list. Father is no exception. He has become the butt of jokes, the fall guy, the well-meaning blunderer. But no matter how much he is tarnished by the comics and the TV sitcoms, he is still revered and loved, though he still may need polishing up.

Now might be a good time for you to take stock of your performance as a father. Answer the items ahead. (Others may rate their fathers or husbands with the quiz).

Dr. Ross Parke (University of Illinois, Urbana) and Dr. Douglas Sawin (University of Texas, Austin), collaborated on studies of just what makes a concerned father. Our test is based on these findings. Answer "Yes" or "No" to each item.

1. More than occasionally, I bypass the chance to eat with the family.
2. I offer much constructive criticism to my kids.
3. A child should know up front what the punishment will be if he/she is disobedient.
4. I manage to find some time to play with my kids each week.
5. I spend a few quiet moments with my children each day at bedtime.
6. As a man, I don't see it as my role to regularly prepare a meal with my kids.
7. A good father teaches mostly by actions, not words.
8. My children often see me show regard and affection for my wife.

ANSWERS

1. No. Being a father means being involved with your kids. If you are seldom at home, it is wise to spend most mealtimes with them even if it's only a snack together.

2. No. Offering constructive criticism is OK, but the trick is to let some foul-ups go by, then bring them up indirectly in a helpful, non-critical way later.

3. No. It's better not to lay down the law before a child actually errs. Let him know that you don't approve of certain actions, but avoid casting the threat of reprisal before he/she acts.

4. Yes. Play is the language of children. Think of playtime as a form of communication. Through play, trust and a wide range of feelings and values can be conveyed.

5. Yes. Bedtime is the time when the "fever" of the day is over and its tempo subsides. It provides the opportunity to share affection and heart-to-heart disclosures.

6. No. A father shouldn't view cooking or meal preparation as non-masculine. It can be a creative fun activity for all.

7. & 8. Yes. Words are not nearly as effective in imparting proper behavior as actions are. An overt deed like hugging your mate or expressing kind words provides a child with a model of behavior. Action is one of the best teaching techniques.

In general, fathers can be just as sensitive and responsive to their children as mothers are, and, if treated properly, children can form strong equal attachments to both parents.

SCORE
4 or 5 is average. If your score is higher than 6, you are doing a very good job of fathering your children. Scores of 3 or less indicate too little involvement with your children. Review the answers for suggestions on how you can contribute more to your child's emotional development.

NOTE: Fathers, who are away a lot, generally have children who, later on, have more trouble in courtships and a less satisfying social life compared with those who are home more often. The general public senses the problem of absent or inaccessible fathers. In a survey of 350,000 of its readers, *Better Homes and Gardens* revealed that an astonishing 87 percent believed that fathers do not spend enough time with their children. Americans seem to accept this as a condition of modern living. A good book on how fathers can influence positive growth in children is *Father Power* by Henry Biller.

WILL YOUR YOUNGSTER BE A LOSER AT SCHOOL?
Eric is a happy, friendly, alert teenager from a stable family. He could easily be the envy of all his friends for he has everything going for him, right? Wrong. You see, Eric happens to be failing at school.

You needn't look far to find a youngster like him in your own neighborhood-one who has all the credentials for climbing to the top of his class, but, in reality , is struggling valiantly to keep up.

Students like this wander into the school counselor's office every day for help. The causes of their dilemma are fairly common. Assuming there are no serious perceptual or cognitive problems like dyslexia or a learning disability the trouble usually lies in several hidden factors, unknown even to the student himself.

You might want to give your child the quiz ahead to see if there are any trouble spots that might hinder his/her school performance. Answer each item yes or no then read on for explanations.

1. You try to record as many notes as possible in class.
2. You usually cram for exams.
3. You would report to the health office if you felt you had a slight fever.
4. You watch TV more than most of your friends do.
5. One or both of your parents dropped out of school.
6. You are unenthusiastic about most of your teachers.
7. You fell in love, or were engaged during the school year.
8. Your school has too many "squares" who would rather follow rules than have fun.
9. You have more brothers than sisters.
10. You would rate your parents as more permissive than average.

SALVATORE V. DIDATO, PH.D.

EXPLANATION

This quiz taps personal attitudes, school habits and home influences that might affect school-work. The items are based on research done at the University of Minnesota and the University of Illinois. Answers that are most likely to predict good school performance follow along with advice and explanations.

1. No. Don't attempt a verbatim transcript of what the teacher says, it will slow you down. Instead, jot down only key ideas and phrases in your own words. Take notes in outline form.

2. No. Although cramming does help to pass exams, your retention will be practically zero several days later.

3. No. Students who avoid classes by easily adopting the "sick role" are more likely than not to be poor students. Many of them respond with a yes to this statement

4. No. Problem students would tend to respond positively to this statement. A common escapist pattern is to watch TV when they should be hitting the books.

5. No. Studies show that if either of your parents has dropped out of school, the chances of your becoming a dropout increase. Such parents must fight against the tendency, unwittingly or not, to foster anti-school attitudes in their youngsters.

6. No. Students who rate their teachers low on performance tend to be low achievers themselves. It smacks of a "sour grapes" outlook blaming others if their work turns out sub-standard.

7. No. Many students who are romantically involved either fail to return to school or do poorly upon returning. Motivation for education drops when love is on one's mind.

8. No. A flunking student is more likely to respond with a yes here, than one who is passing. Generally, he feels most people around him are out of step but not he.

9. Yes. Achievement will be better if you have more brothers than sisters. Some parents tend to stress education for boys somewhat more than education for girls and one's family atmosphere will reflect this attitude.

10. No. Permissive parents have a tendency to sway their youngsters toward permissiveness about their school duties. Too often this turns into laxity and then, failing grades.

SCORE

Take a point for each correct answer and rate yourself as follows:

6 or more points. You have constructive features operating in your situation and probably will do better than average this term.

4-5 points. You have an average balance among the factors and should do at least average work, providing you stick to it.

0-3 points. You probably have some hidden aspects in your personality or environment that will make school difficult for you. You'll have t try harder to get through. Consider seeking the help of a guidance officer if you're having trouble.

CAN YOU SPOT A CHILD UNDER STRESS?

Who can forget that poignant picture by *Parade* magazine photographer Eddie Adams of a naked, weeping child fleeing an attack in an embattled area of Vietnam? No one knows how the experience shaped the child's personality. What we do know is that the stress of war leaves telling scars on children, whether in Ireland, the Middle East or southeast Asia.

Although there is much distance between the anguished Vietnamese girl and our own children, there may be psychological similarities; children everywhere face daily stress "wars" that have an impact on their development.

According to Dr. David Elkind, chairman of the Department of Child Study at Tufts University in Massachusetts, children today are pressured into social, psychological and political maturity too quickly, and the resulting stress may have long-lasting, damaging effects. Evidence of this may be found in the fact that during the past decade the number of children seen by psychologists and psychiatrists has increased five-fold. And when children have no other way of venting their feelings, some choose suicide.

According to FBI statistics, about 14 suicides occur daily among children between ages of 10 and 19 nationwide.

We reel under the crush of articles and books on adult stress, but too little is said about children.

Have you ever considered how much stress your children, or children you know, may be enduring and how it affects them?

Following is a list of 20 stressful situations. The list is adapted from Elkind's book *The Hurried Child*. To identify how much stress a child has been under, check each item that the child you know has experienced within the past year.

1. Parent dies 10
2. Parents divorce 7
3. Parents separate 6
4. Parent travels for business 6
5. Close family member dies 6
6. Parent remarries 5
7. Parent fired from job 4.5
8. Parents reconcile 4.5
9. Mother begins work outside home 4.5
10. Health of family member changes 4.5
11. Mother becomes pregnant 4
12. A sibling is born 4
13. Family's financial condition changes 4
14. Number of fights with siblings changes 3.5
15. Responsibilities at home change 3
16. Older brother or sister leaves home 3

17. Trouble occurs with grandparents 3
18. Move to another neighborhood or city takes place 2
19. Family goes on vacation 2
20. Number of family get-togethers changes 1.5

SCORING AND EXPLANATIONS

To tally the child's score, total the numbers given to the right of each item you checked.

0-9.5 is average and indicates that a child has a relatively tranquil life. There is a good chance that children with this score will achieve their full potential, free of personal hang-ups.

10-18 indicates that the child will have more of a tendency to develop some symptom of stress than children who receive an average score.

19 or more indicates a heavy stress load and a strong chance that this child will undergo a fairly serious change in health and/or behavior.

The late Dr. Hans Selye of McGill University in Montreal, who is known for his theory of stress, emphasized that stress occurs when we adapt to any event in our life. Thus, it doesn't matter if the incident is a happy one or a sad one; the fact that we must make an adjustment to it produces stress. For example, it may be just as stressful for a child to be outstanding in personal achievement as it is to adjust to an older sibling leaving home.

Unlike most adults, children under stress usually don't express their feelings verbally. Rather, they tend to act out with behavior such as bed-wetting, nail biting, nightmares, seclusiveness, aggression, inattention and stuttering. Therefore, clues that children are experiencing too much stress can be found in their behavior.

DO YOU HAVE GOOD PARENT SMARTS?

It was a child psychologist Bruno Bettelheim who once said that love is not enough to raise an emotionally healthy child. What the founder of the famous Orthogenic School for Children in Chicago meant was that a parent's love is important, of course, but even the most loving of us makes mistakes that will adversely affect our children.

Raising a child is a responsibility that no human being is innately equipped to handle. And with new methods of child-rearing cropping up every few years, it may be difficult to know how best to guide a child.

What do good parents do for their children? Professor James V. McConnell (University of Michigan) who researched mother-child relationships, states that, among other things, the good parent trains the child to respond in acceptable ways by lavishing love and attention on him when he is good and by disciplining him and withholding affection when he is not. But the point is, there may be vast differences between spouses on the issue of what behavior is acceptable and unacceptable.

If you are a parent or hope to be one what misconceptions might you have that could hamper your child's healthy growth?

Answer the items ahead "yes" or "no". They are based on McConnell's and other studies.

1. Schools have the prime responsibility of helping children to mature.

2. My display of love for my children is much influenced by how good they are at the time.

3. It is difficult for me to discuss sex, drugs, suicide, etc., with my kids.

4. I regularly take the time to discuss personal issues with each child individually.

5. I believe it's healthy to show my feelings honestly, so it wouldn't bother me to praise or scold my child in front of his siblings or friends.

6. Kids should be given a sense of independence as soon as possible, even if it means they might endure painful defeats now and then.

7. I rarely discuss controversial subjects because it might cause arguments.

8. I show my children that I'm on their wavelength and very much like one of their peers.

ANSWERS

Take a point for each answer that matches those ahead.

1. No. It may be true that teachers influence a child, but the major responsibility of shaping a child's character rests with parents.

2. No. It might be hard sometimes to show love when frustrated with a naughty child, but the art of parenting is to show disapproval while at the same time projecting an underlying feeling of love for the errant child.

3. No. A child is not at fault for raising questions about any topic. Rather, it is the insecure parent who labels it a "taboo" and then proceeds to avoid its discussion. Even if a parent is uncomfortable, something should be said no matter how general, about a subject that a child is curious about.

4. Yes. Kids deserve special time alone with Mom and/or Dad. It's wise to respect their individuality and recognize that each child poses unique questions about life.

5. No. A good rule is not to scold in front of others, but to praise in the presence of others.

6. No. Giving independence is a noble gesture but not always in a child's best interests. Independence might be granted to a child because of a parent's weakness or indecisiveness. Before freedom is granted, be reasonably certain that no pronounced harm would follow.

7. No. Arguments can be constructive if they are controlled, fair and generate more light than heat. A good parent can use the discussion of controversial subjects to enlighten his child on important issues.

8. No. It's a mistake to abandon your role as parent for the sake of convincing your children that you are similar to them. A child should never feel that you're like his peers, There are other ways to show that you empathize with him without relinquishing your authority role, such as sharing fun activity and making joint decisions.

SCORE

Consider a score of 4 or 5 average. If your score is higher than 6, you are doing a good job of parenting. If your score is 3 or less, review the explanations here and in the "Concerned Mother" and "Concerned Father" tests for ways to boost your parent role and form a more nurturing positive relationship with your kids.

WIFE: WHAT'S YOUR IRRITABILITY INDEX?

A housewife is a woman who does what no one ever notices unless she doesn't do it well. In the line of battle, she faces unexpected domestic situations every hour on the hour. She is constantly under fire to solve problems, some small, some large but all irritating. It takes a flexible and adaptable personality to succeed in the world's most challenging job, but even the best of them lose composure now and then.

Below is a test of irritability. It involves situations which might confront an average housewife. Both husband and wife should take the quiz then compare scores.

Use the 3-point scale below to rank each situation in terms of how irritated it would make you feel. You may find some difficult to rate, but try honestly to come up with the rating which describes most accurately, how you would react if the situation actually happened to you.

RANKING

Slight irritation 1
Moderate irritation 2
Strong irritation 3

1. Your husband calls you and says he'll be home in 15 minutes with 2 important business associates. You will have to cancel your weekly movie with friends, tidy up the house, and then fix a meal for all of you.

2. Your small son tears his expensive suit jacket moments before you are to leave for a wedding reception. It's the only thing for him to wear and you must take an hour to sew it, and you'll all walk in late at the affair.

3. You suddenly notice water dripping from the ceiling on your expensive drapes. You investigate and find that someone (not you) left the bath water running and overflowed the tub.

4. You are wearing an expensive cocktail dress at a party you're having for some very style-conscious friends. A couple of close friends whisper to you that the hem you sewed on the dress is far too wide, possibly by 2 inches.

5. You are completing a strawberry shortcake for guests arriving in five minutes. After the first layer of luscious berries, the remainder in the basket are crushed and rotten. The grocer assured you "they are all perfect" but he's closed now and you don't have anything else to serve.

6. It is broiling hot out. Your air conditioner, going at full blast all day, hasn't been cooling off the house, as it should. You discover that someone left a large window open behind a drape where it couldn't be seen.

7. A careless but dear neighbor asks to borrow your sewing machine for a few days. Once she borrowed your electric fry pan and jammed it with so much grease, it cost you $29 to repair. She's done you many favors and you can't say no to her.

8. Your young daughter refuses to eat her lunch. You're very annoyed. In walks your (usually critical) mother-in-law. You step into the next room to take a lengthy phone call and when you return, you find that she has succeeded in getting your daughter to eat every single scrap of food plus an additional glass of milk and several cookies to boot.

9. You are expecting a sofa to be delivered by 11 AM. You have an important meeting to attend at 2 PM. The sofa is finally delivered by 4:30 PM and you had to miss the meeting. The deliverymen didn't call to say they'd be late. If they did you could have easily made the meeting and returned home in time to receive the sofa.

10. You've been up half the night caring for your 9-year-old son's poison ivy rash. A few days ago, you warned him not to play in the woods, but he didn't listen to you.

Now tote up the score and find your rating as follows:

SCORE
    10-16 Low irritability level
    17-23 Moderate irritability level
    24-30 High irritability level

How does your rating compare with that of your spouse?

Since adaptability to a trying situation goes hand in hand with your irritation level, the more irritated you are the less you are likely to be adaptable. The virtue of patience in times of stress calls for emotional control. That is what maturity is. Experiments show that when a person loses his composure and goes out of control, his ability for problem-solving is severely reduced. Also, B. von Haller Gilmer, of the Carnegie Institute of Technology, verified that constant irritability can lead to "irritable aggression" which, of course, is an outcome to be avoided. So if you want to increase your effectiveness as a housewife try to maintain your calm.

Note: The tests here and ahead, are similar to those used to assess frustration tolerance in married couples.

HUSBAND: WHAT'S YOUR IRRITABILITY INDEX ?

A man once introduced his wife to a group by saying, "Here is the little lady who helps me out of all the frustrating situations I would never have gotten into had I not married her in the first place." This type of scapegoating in the battle of the sexes is perennial, but in the final analysis, unproductive for happy unions. Wise marriage mates are able to (1) accept responsibility for causing their own irritation; (2) foresee those situations which will provoke their irritation; and, (3) take steps together to avoid such scenarios or exercise emotional control over them.

Although both husband and wife have many irritations in common, each may respond quite differently to the same circumstances because of different value systems.

Below is a quiz which will determine your overall irritability level. It deals with events which might confront an average husband. Both husband and wife should take it, then compare scores. Each should try to predict how the other would react.

Instructions:

Using the 3-point scale below, rank each situation in terms of how irritated it would make you feel. You may find some difficult to rate, but try honestly to come up with the rating which describes most accurately just how you would react if the event actually happened to you.

Slight irritation 1
Moderate irritation 2
Strong irritation 3

1. Your dull razor won't cut your tough beard. You have 15 minutes to prepare for a party. You asked your wife to buy some blades three days ago. She forgot. She suggests you get to the drug store before it closes. You race over and arrive just as he's locking the door. After a bit of pleading, he leads you back in, but you find he's completely out of all blades.

2. Your 16 year-old son forgot to roll up your car windows as you'd asked and its seats are thoroughly soaked after an all night rain. You must pick up the men in your car pool in a few minutes.

3. You search for the evening paper which has an important article in it which you haven't read yet. You discover that your wife cleaned some fish and used the paper to catch up the slop.

4. Your wife finally calls in a carpenter to do a simple job you've been putting off for weeks. The bill comes to $48.

5. You're low on gas but decide to try to make it home without stopping at a station. About seven miles from home, on a lonely road, you run out of gas. 25 minutes later, a driver finally stops, smiles coolly, and offers you a ride. It's a neighbor with whom you've had some frictions from time to time, but you accept the lift home anyway.

6. You try to phone home all afternoon to tell your wife that because of an emergency, you'll be working late and to cancel a dinner party with two other couples at your home. You can't get through because your 15 year-old daughter is on the phone all the time. By now the hungry guests have begun to arrive.

7. You and the family are lost for one and a half hours on a hot, dusty road because you agreed to follow your wife's directions to a friend's house she said she knew 'by heart'. You try to make a 'U' turn on a narrow road but slip into a ditch and get stuck. Your wife starts to berate you for your 'poor judgment' in attempting such a turn.

8. Your 8 year-old son has never been fishing. You've been eagerly looking forward to the joy of taking him yourself for the first time to share with him the excitement of his new experience, but you've been busy lately. That evening he happily greets you and says how glad he is that his mother allowed him to go fishing with a neighbor.

9. A new neighbor phones to ask that you remove your car from in front of his driveway. You reply that you will. You're actually only about 14 inches over the line and if he were to take his car out, he could squeeze past yours if he were careful. The whole matter slips your mind and half an hour later a police officer rings your bell and directs you to move the car or get a ticket.

10. You dine at an excellent restaurant, but, in a way, you resent its high prices. When you tally the bill, you observe that you weren't charged for two glasses of wine. Your first impulse is to pay the bill as is and forget the omission, but your wife urges you to mention it. You do, since you feel it can't come to much more than $7 or $8 a glass. When the corrected bill arrives, the wine costs a total of $39.

Now total up the score and find what it means.

Rank Score

10-16 Low irritability level

17-23 Moderate irritability level

24-30 High irritability level

How does your rating compare with that of your spouse?

Your effectiveness as a husband, or for that matter, as a person, goes hand in hand with your irritation level. The more frustrated you become, the less likely that you will be adaptable to problem situations. Experiments show that when a person loses emotional control, his problem-solving ability is sharply reduced.

Leslie Born and his team at McMaster University, Ontario has researched our topic using questionnaires and found similar results. Also, G.L. Freeman and associates at Northwestern University learned that a constant irritable state and the muscle tension it produces could easily lead to physical symptoms

Generally speaking, then, if you can keep calm, you will come out ahead in life's stressful moments.

CAN YOU "PSYCHE OUT" A CHILD'S MIND?

"The child is father to the man." This is a basic truth about children, namely, that they show signs of what they will become. Many, but not all, of the traits a child will develop are a direct influence of its parents and family members. Understandably, through many years of interaction, youngsters develop the basic core of their personality.

But life often moves so fast that we don't take time out to examine important factors which shape their behavior. Do you take for granted certain half-truths handed down to you and hope that somehow your most precious possessions will grow into wholesome individuals?

The quiz probes your knowledge about kids. Mark each item true or false, some answers may surprise you.

1. My child will learn to talk more rapidly if I habitually repeat the word he tries to say.
2. Right-handers show better judgment and reasoning than do left-handers.
3. In important matters, children shouldn't question their parent's judgment.
4. Basically, most kids really want their parents to give them more freedom than they have.
5. It is instinctive for children to love their parents.
6. If I make fairly strong demands for achievement early in the life of my child, it will create too much anxiety in him.
7. The smaller my family, the greater the chance that my child will be emotionally stable.
8. Young children who are hard to manage, usually respond well to more discipline.

EXPLANATION

1. False. It probably won't help much to incessantly drill your child in word usage. Children learn language almost entirely without direct instruction.

2. False. More than 2000 students at Cambridge University, England, were given mental tests and no differences in reasoning and judgment were found between right and left-handers.

3. False. Parents who don't feel threatened by allowing their kids to pose sincere questions about their decisions tend to raise self-reliant and responsible kids provided there is mutual respect on both sides.

4. False. In a poll of some 27,000 students, the National Institute of Student Opinion found that 66% wanted their parents to be somewhat strict with them, compared with 33% who wanted less discipline.

5. False. Love is not innately determined; rather it is an emotion of human experience which is acquired. A child learns to love those who show love to him, i.e., those who provide care, food, hugging, etc.

6. False. Research by Harvard University psychologists shows that the earlier the parental demand for reasonable achievement, the stronger the subsequent drive for achievement, provided the child has a good relationship with its parents.

7. True. Studies by psychologist Ross Stagner of Wayne State University showed that there is a tendency for small families to produce children who are more emotionally adjusted than those who come from larger families. The differences, however, are not overwhelmingly great. In large families, parents will have to try harder to provide emotional support to all their offspring.

8. False. Although fair discipline is necessary, much of the difficulty might possibly be corrected by a more perceptive mother. Work at the University of Wisconsin, showed that mothers who describe their toddlers as "difficult" were the ones who showed low awareness of the needs of a distressed infant shown to them on video. These mothers need more help in developing sensitivity to their child's needs.

SCORE
Consider that a score of at least 3 correct is average.

WHAT IS YOUR MARRIAGE STYLE?
No two people are alike and, though the words "you are now joined together as one" are a central idea in marriage ceremonies, seldom are both mates exactly alike in personality. Rather, any close bond is a blend of two points of view about life, a blend that will or will not work depending upon how tolerant each member is of the other's outlook.

Clifford J. Sager, a clinical professor of psychiatry at Mt. Sinai Medical School in New York, has studied various basic types of relations. In his book, *Marriage Contracts*, he stresses that each marriage has a personality, just as each person has. There are a cluster of traits and predictable reaction patterns that make a marriage unique.

Our quiz is based on Sager's research. To learn what your relationship style is, check the items which best describe you and your partner. Please limit yourself to only four or five best choices.

1. For the most part, you are both similar in neatness habits, food, music and movie tastes.
2. You both like to do things together, such as play cards, swim, garden, play tennis, etc.
3. You share thoughts and feelings about a wide range of experiences, such as how you feel about friends, a good joke, a pretty sunset or a news article.
4. You both equally like to give and receive physical affection.
5. One partner doesn't particularly care to do something that must be done, such as drive, grocery shop, devise a budget, while the other doesn't mind or may even enjoy it.
6. One partner is a good talker; the other is a good listener.
7. One partner is outgoing the other is reserved.
8. One is competitive, the other is not.
9. You both have contrasting opinions on matters such as politics, religion, and social issues.
10. You differ sharply in your choice of friends.
11. When you differ on an issue, such as where to vacation, how to spend money or whose parents to visit, there is usually a heated controversy before a decision is made.
12. You differ strongly about how to enjoy an evening, with one preferring, for example, a movie to a party, an art exhibit to dancing, etc.

EXPLANATION

There are three basic inter-actional styles:

1. **The Harmonious Couple**. If most of your choices were among items 1 through 4 then your relationship is one of harmony You see each other as one with whom to share life experiences rather than a rival to be conquered. This couple has an excellent chance for a rich and solid future. But, beware sometimes apparently harmonious teams can clash when the agreement between them is phony. Some couples pretend to agree out of fear of dealing directly with their differences.

2. **The Complementary Couple**. If your choices were mostly for items 5 and 6, you are in a complimentary relationship. You both meet each other's needs by filling out the other's personality. Sometimes, such couples seem an odd match, i.e., he's a scientist, and she's an artist. But when complementary behavior simply bolsters a partner's weakness, it won't lead to growth for either party. For example, if you're shy about confronting others and your mate usually takes over this task for you, your mate's "support" may block you from ever learning to assert yourself.

3. **The Conflicting or Competitive Couple**. Checks for items 9 through 12 disclose a conflicting or competitive bond. Your needs are in opposition and you are like a couple on a ladder who climb over each other to reach the top when there is only enough room for one on each rung. This style isn't as beneficial as the other two, but it need not be destructive. Greater damage occurs when couples hide their differences. Not expressing conflicting ideas often blocks mutual understanding of your true needs and wishes. Also, because competitive couples are so willing to express their individual opinions and needs, they can use this communication to forge an agreement where possible and come to mutually satisfying compromises where necessary.

So, what's your style?

No one style guarantees perfect happiness. Most of us show a blend of each inter-actional pattern. though one may dominate. The upshot is that no matter what your style, the joy in your relationship is a matter of what you make it.

"It's of a personal nature."

CHAPTER 4
GETTING ALONG WITH OTHERS

HOW WELL DO YOU HANDLE DISAGREEMENTS?

When you tangle with someone who's disagreeable, how do you deal with it? Are you a loser because you lack the right finesse when coping with interpersonal conflict?

Psychologists have classified people according to how they cope with disagreement. Research began some 60 years ago when companies devised methods for forming smooth-running, efficient groups in their organizations. Such "team building" techniques have made companies much happier places in which to work.

To answer the question "How do you handle conflicts?" take the following quiz. It is based on the work of industrial psychologists

Robert R. Blake and Jane S. Mouton, who produced the "managerial grid," a method for evaluating the styles executives use to cope with discord. They did their research while at the University of Texas.

TRUE OR FALSE:

1. Most of the time I give in to those who argue with me.

2. In most arguments, I am generally quite firm in pursuing my side of the issue.

3. I avoid disagreements by steering clear of controversial topics such as religion, politics, etc.

4. I use my influence on others to get my ideas accepted.

5. I usually keep my conflicts and hard feelings to myself.

6. When I'm at odds with people, I don't call them, rather I usually wait until they phone me first.

7. Many of the difficulties people get into are self-caused.

8. I like to ask questions which are hard for others to answer.

9. I'd rather not have the headaches that come with a leadership post.

10. I like to instruct people on how to do things.

11. It makes me uncomfortable when others do small demeaning tasks and errands for me.

12. At meetings, I have a fairly strong need to make sure my point of view is heard.

EXPLANATION:

There are two basic styles of handling interpersonal conflicts: concern for self and concern for others. The first describes the person who attempts to come out a winner and satisfy his/her own concerns (all even numbered items refer to this style). The second describes a person who wants to be conciliatory and satisfy the needs of others (all odd numbered items indicate this approach). Most people use a style of settling problems that is a blend of the two dimensions.

The particular style in which power over others takes is a learned behavior. Children who grow up in families where disputes are settled through power plays, subtle or overt, tend to adopt similar patterns when they grow up. *

SCORE:
The more you answered True to the even numbered items rather than the odd numbered items, the more you handle interpersonal frictions as a dominant, self-focused person. If your answers were True to more of the odd numbered items, then you use a more obliging style of resolving clashes with others. An average person would answer True or False to approximately equal numbers of dominant and obliging items.

NOTE:
In dealing with superiors or those above us in status or rank, we usually say what will be received as acceptable rather than what we believe is true. That's obvious enough. It's expected that we will more likely use a more compliant style with superiors than with peers and more with peers than subordinates. When people are equal in power, they tend to use a compromising style in settling their quarrels. Their drive to win in a dispute is more a need for personal glory rather than to achieve a group goal. On the other hand, in business for example, some workers have a genuine liking for conquests. They enjoy directing and swaying others, controlling situations and coming out on top. David McClelland of Harvard, whose work on team building is well known, sees this as a healthy motivation when it is used to attain group objectives and is a trait of good managers.

As far as genders go, the evidence is that males are more dominating and less obliging than females in conflict situations.

* Societies differ in the style of power plays. Author Michael Korda, author of the book *Power*, says it succinctly: "The contemporary American style is to pretend one has none. To confess that one has power is to make oneself responsible for using it and safety lies in an artfully contrived pose of impotence behind which one can do exactly as one pleases".

WHAT DO BODY GESTURES REVEAL? PART 1
Though words are man's crowning achievement, communicating to others also depends upon the actions and postures of our "talking bodies." The most well known human gesture of our time was flashed by Winston Churchill who, during World War II, raised two fingers in a V for victory sign and instantly communicated to millions the essence of a powerful message. Other more universal gestures include the hitchhiker's thumb up, the temple tap to indicate one who is mentally unbalanced, and the hand wave use both as a greeting and a farewell.

Human gestures have now become a part of a much larger body of knowledge called kinesics, the study of body language and psychiatry has gained much from these new insights. With these findings, professionals in mental health can approximate the inner feelings of clients who are either unwilling or unable to convey their attitudes with words.

Although there are a growing number of kinesiologists, who study body language, there are practically none who examine specific gestures as such. Four British scholars at Oxford did one recent and outstanding study. In their book, *Gestures*, D. Morris, P. Collett, P. Marsh, and M. O'Shaughnessy, report on the results of extensive geographical surveys throughout Europe involving some 1,200 people. Their goal was to study the universality of various gestures.

Test your knowledge of the subject. The 5 gestures illustrated convey specific meanings. Next to each numbered picture, choose a corresponding meaning from those ahead, then check your answers.

1. The Fingertip Kiss

2. The Hand Purse

3. The Vertical Horn Sign

4. The Cheek Screw

5. The Fingers Cross

POSSIBLE GESTURE MEANINGS

    A. Disinterest

    B. Anger

    C. Praise, excellence

    D. Protection

    E. Query; I ask

    F. Good

    G. He is cuckold

ANSWERS / EXPLANATION

    1 C; 2 E; 3 G; 4 F; 5 D.

    1. The fingertip kiss is a symbolic version of a mouth kiss, which is estimated to be over 2,000 years old. It is recorded that the Greeks and Romans threw a kiss toward the deity when they left their temples of worship. Through the years it has come to mean approval and praise.

    2. The hand purse was as first mentioned in 1932 in Europe. Bringing the fingers together in a point means to bring ideas together, thus, it is a request for someone to come to the point and bring forth an answer.

    3. The vertical horn sign is a gross insult to a man. It says that his wife has been unfaithful.

    4. The cheek screw is often a gesture used to say that food is good. It points to the teeth, and the Italian expression *al dente*, "on the tooth," means that something is just right for eating.

    5. The fingers cross is a carryover of a religious gesture symbolizing the cross. Instead of crossing himself openly, a Christian could project himself as not evil and avoid capture by making a cross with his fingers.

SCORE

Most persons should get at least 3 correct on this test.

WHAT DO BODY GESTURES REVEAL, PART 2

If inept waiters frustrate you, then you and Dr. Allan Mazur have something in common. The Syracuse University sociologist uses a tactic that seems to work well for him. "It's all a matter of how you use your body language," the professor explains. When he wants careless waiters to pay more attention to him, Mazur simply avoids looking at them when they speak to him. This, he explains, is a subtle way of exerting your status over someone.

    Body gestures often deliver subtle shades of feeling that words may fail to express, although through the centuries, gestures were traditionally considered a secondary, trivial form of human communication. But over a century ago, no less a giant of science than Charles Darwin took note of the special significance of gestures. He commented on the "shoulder shrug gesture," which involves a raised brow, an open mouth, a tilted head and bent forearms with palms in. He regarded this gesture as a nearly universal expression of uncertainty, impotence or resignation, and even went so far as to declare that the shoulder shrug could be an innate human response.

Research on cultural gestures has been sparse. Recently, however, four Oxford University psychologists, on a grant from the Guggenheim Foundation in New York, conducted an extensive survey of 25 European countries. Their mission: to construct a "gestures map" that would show the most popular gestures utilized by various nationalities in their communication patterns.

Test yourself on gesture meanings by taking the quiz below. It is based upon the work of the Oxford team namely D. Morris, P. Collett, P. Marsh and M. O'Shaughnessy and found in their book, "Gestures"

From the list of possible meanings, pick out the five correct ones to match the gestures pictured, then read on for explanations.

Possible Gesture Meanings

A. Scorn or "I will give nothing"

B. He is a cuckhold

C. He or she is thin, ill

D. Don't believe what you hear

E. He is effeminate

F. Keep it secret, be wary

G. He or she is jealous

1. The Horizontal Horn Sign

2. The Cheek Stroke

3. The Teeth Flick

4. The Ear Touch

5. The Nose Tap

GESTURES, PART 2

ANSWERS

1. B; 2. C; 3. A; 4. E; 5. F

EXPLANATIONS

1. The horizontal horn sign goes back to pre-Roman times (2,500 years or more). It ridicules a man and tells that his wife has cheated on him. Originally it was a device for protection, a meaning it still retains somewhat. It reflects an old practice of hanging animal horns in a home to protect it from evil.

2. The cheek stroke is found mostly in southeast Europe, and it first appeared in the early 19th century. Slight pressure on the cheek conveys the image of a haggard and emaciated person. Often, if the cheeks are not pressed, it could indicate that someone to whom the gesturer refers is attractive.

3. The teeth flick has two meanings, namely that the gesturer does not care or will give nothing (not the skin of his teeth). It also shows scorn or anger. It probably originated in England as biting the thumb and is often mentioned by Shakespeare. For example, in *Romeo and Juliet*, Sampson says: "I will bite my thumb at them; which is a disgrace to them."

4. The ear touch is widely recognized as a sexual slur on a man. Touching the earlobe says, in effect, "He ought to wear earrings like a woman." It could be an outright accusation of being homosexual.

5. The message of the nose tap is: "We have sniffed something out, let's keep it to ourselves." A "noser" in England is slang for a police informer. When a criminal taps his nose he means "Keep silent, there is a noser nearby."

The quiz demonstrates that a human gesture is a body picture that often can be well worth a thousand words. So next time someone remarks, "I see what you mean," be reminded that he or she is absorbing more than just your words.

SCORE

Most people should get at lease 3 correct on this test.

WHAT DO BODY GESTURES REVEAL, PART 3

Very little had been done on the meaning of gestures until a few years ago when a breakthrough was made by several behavior scientists at Oxford University in England. Morris, Collett, Marsh and O'Shaughnessy conducted a worldwide survey throughout 25 countries in the Eastern hemisphere to find common meanings that people held for a number of well-known gestures. Some of the countries in which they interviewed over 1,200 subjects included

Scotland, Holland, Denmark, France, Italy, Spain and Tunisia. When they finished their enormous task of "gesture mapping," their findings were published in a book, *'Gestures'* (Stein & Day, New York). They conclude that gestures are a language in and of themselves. They are "body pictures," if you will, and some countries, like Italy and Spain, rely upon them more than others (England and Sweden).

The authors point out those societies that do not utilize body gestures are at a disadvantage in that they do not enjoy the fullest range of communicative versatility.

What is your "gesture IQ"? Below are 5 gestures studied by the Oxford team. Match them up with their specific meanings then read on for answers and explanations.

1. The Head Toss

2. The Chin Flick

3. The Flat-Hand Flick

4. The Fig

5. The Eyelid Pull

POSSIBLE GESTURE MEANINGS

    A. Mockery

    B. I depart, he departs

    C. Sexual insult

    D. Keep it secret

    E. No, negative reaction

    F. Let us be alert

    G. Disinterest

ANSWERS

    1 E; 2 G; 3 B; 4 C; 5 F.

EXPLANATIONS

    1. The head toss is a silent "no" and a variation of the side-to-side head shake. It is practically a universally accepted gesture. According to evolutionist Charles Darwin, moving the head to indicate a "no" reaction is a human signal that originates in the infant's primary act of rejecting food, for when a baby refuses to eat, it will turn its head from side to side to avoid being fed.

    2. The chin flick gesture originates largely with the French who named it "la barbe" (the beard). Symbolically it is a beard flick and a simple insult in which the gesturer flips his imaginary beard to say buzz off, shut up, get lost, don't bother me.

    3. The flat-hand flick has two parts; the flicked right hand shows something going away from the gesturer and the chopping down action of the left hand amplifies this by severing the right hand. Together these show some kind of departure. It can be a command like "go away" or a comment like "he's gone" or "please move on."

    4. The fig symbolizes male and female genitalia but to display this gesture is usually a reference to female sexuality. Often it connotes the idea of wanting to make love to a woman.

    5. The eyelid pull follows a simple action of widening the eye to increase awareness. Often it means that the gesturer is saying, "I'm on the lookout and I am wary" or "you can't fool me."

    A score of 3 or better is average for this test.

WILL VIRTUE BE REWARDED? (DO YOU BELIEVE IN A JUST WORLD?)

There are people who repeatedly come upon hard times. They stumble from one tragedy to another asking themselves, "Why me?" They encounter so many defeats that they could properly be called "victims." Would they suffer so much if they changed their way of living? Is their fate dependent on their actions or is it predestined? Some believe that we make our own luck, while others hold steadfastly to the idea that victims have been dealt a bad hand. Which do you believe?

The following quiz measures how you feel about victims and their fate. Answer each item "true" or "false." Then read on for explanations.

1. In America, where opportunity abounds, if one is a beggar he has brought on his own fate.

2. Most people who allow themselves to suffer do so to gain sympathy.

3. People who fail and then blame it on bad luck are usually responsible for their own downfall.

4. Patients who refuse to follow a doctor's advice shouldn't expect sympathy if they get sick.

5. People who lose consistently often bite off more than they can chew.

6. People who live good, moral lives usually have fewer setbacks than those who don't.

7. Most rape victims could have possibly avoided it by dressing more conservatively, being more careful about where they socialize and returning home at a decent hour.

8. Most drivers who have accidents are careless or selfish while driving.

9. I probably wouldn't pity a formerly rich man who has lost all his money.

10. It is common for a guilty person to be found innocent in American courts.

EXPLANATION

These quiz items gauge your attitude about victims. Do you think that victims deserve their fate? Do you feel compassion for them? Or are you somewhere between the extremes of a bleeding heart and a hard nose?

In the comics. Sad Sack, that born loser, was loved by all; but in real life it's another matter. The fact is, we don't want to be like the underdog. Rather, we identify with a winner and want to do what he does.

The topic of justice for victims has been studied extensively by Melvin Lerner, professor of psychology at Waterloo University in Canada. He finds that people see a link between virtue and reward. No matter how understanding we are, some of us tend to blame victims for their own bad breaks. A prevalent notion is that if we are perfectly fair, honest, responsible, etc., then we will be spared bad luck. This is called the "just-world" attitude, whereby people believe that society is a just place in which to live and each one gets what he deserves.

Psychologist Fritz Heider of Lawrence, Ks., put it succinctly: "The relationship between goodness and happiness, between wickedness and punishment is so strong that given one of these conditions, the other is frequently assumed."

SCORE

To learn to what degree you believe the world is a "just" place, give yourself 1 point for each "true" response you gave to items 1 through 9, and for a "false" response to item 10.

8-10 points. You strongly believe that the world is a just place and that right makes might. Luck has little to do with success or failure You staunchly hold people responsible for their own destiny.

5-7 points. You're on middle ground and believe that one's life is a combination of free choice and good or bad luck.

4 or fewer points. You're quite firm in your belief that people have little control over their welfare and that they are pretty much the victims of circumstance.

NOTE: Lerner has made an interesting finding about our reaction to a victim we encounter and try to help. According to his research, we tend to like a victim who is helped by our efforts. However, if it turns out that we fail to aid or rescue the person, we tend to lose some sympathy for him, dislike him and might even go so far as to blame him for his own suffering.

DO YOU HAVE AN AGE BIAS? PARTS 1 & 2

The National Center for Health Statistics in Washington, D.C., reported recently that 80 percent of the aged people over 70 are healthy enough to carry on normal activities. Consider this one more bit of evidence to shatter some of the myths we have about older persons.

If you are often at a loss to explain the actions or thinking of an aging loved one, here's a chance to discover whether your confusion is caused by mistaken notions. The following items are adapted from various studies. Answer each true or false, then read on for explanations.

Older people:

1. Have little interest in sexual relations.
2. Are often bored.
3. Are lonely and isolated from others.
4. Are set in their ways and usually unable to change.
5. Tend to become more religious as they age.
6. Generally, couples tend to become more alike as they grow older.
7. Feel miserable most of the time.
8. Don't work as well as younger employees.

ANSWERS AND EXPLANATIONS

All answers are false. Give yourself one point for each false answer.

1. Sex researchers Masters and Johnson, of the Reproductive Biology Research Foundation in St. Louis, Mo., report that for most people, the sex drive continues well into the 70s and 80s. In addition to continued interest in intercourse, there is the capacity to perform satisfactorily.

2. Surveys done by Professor Erdman Palmore of Duke University show that although the elderly aren't as active as they were when younger, they are seldom bored. Only 17 percent of those over 65 say that they didn't have enough to keep them busy.

3. About two-thirds of the elderly surveyed in the Duke study say they are never or seldom lonely. Their contacts with relatives and friends are more frequent than commonly believed.

SALVATORE V. DIDATO, PH.D.

4. Most older people adapt to major life changes, such as retirement, widowhood and moving. Their social and political attitudes also shift as society changes, but these changes occur more slowly.

5. Longitudinal studies find no increase in the religious interests of the elderly as they get older.

6. There is as much difference between older individuals as there is between people at any age. In fact, there is evidence that as we grow older we tend to become less alike on many levels.

7. Studies of happiness and life satisfaction published by the Russell Sage Foundation of New York show no significant difference by age groups on these factors. Only 20 to 33 percent of those questioned ranked low on various happiness or morale scales.

8. Sociologists M. Riley and A. Foner, of the National Institutes of Health in Washington, D.C., report that among the 12 percent of the elderly who continue working, the majority are as effective as younger employees. Although they do not work as fast on projects that require speed, their consistency of output increases with age and they have less job turnover, fewer accidents and less absenteeism than their younger co-workers.

Based on Palmore's research, if you answered one or two of the items true, you have an average number of mistaken notions about the elderly. If you answered three or more of the items true, you have above-average age bias.

DO YOU HAVE AN AGE BIAS? PART 2

We're growing healthier and living longer. Today, one out of five Americans is 65 or older. We are entering what has been called an "Age of Gerontocracy."

Do you harbor any false notions when it comes to judging the elderly? Erdman B. Palmore, professor of medical sociology at the Center for the Study of Aging and Human Development (Duke University), has studied the personalities of those over 65 years of age for more than 15 years. The following quiz is based on his findings. Answer True or False to each.

1. Most seniors have defective memories, difficulty in concentrating and show signs of mental inadequacy.

2. Senior citizens tend to be irritated and angry more often than younger persons.

3. There are more acute short-term illnesses among persons over 65 than among those younger.

4. As people get older, they tend to be absent from work more often.

5. When the last child leaves home, most older parents have serious "separation anxiety" problems adjusting to their "empty nest."

6. There are more home accidents among the aged than among those younger.

7. Few people over 60 have the drive or stamina to hold public office.

8. Most older persons live alone.

ANSWERS (All items are FALSE)

1. Many surveys show that fewer than 10 percent of the aged suffer from any mental inadequacies.

2. Over 50 percent of the aged who were polled said they are never or hardly ever angry or irritated and this proportion increases to two-thirds by age 80.

3. According to the National Center for Health Statistics (Washington, D.C.) in 1978 there were 102 acute illnesses per 1000 persons over the age 65 compared with 230 for those under that age. The aged do, however, have a higher proportion of chronic disorders yearly.

4. Seniors have an absentee rate equal to those in middle age (3.2 days per 100), but the rate is lower than for workers under the age 32, who have a rate of 4.2 days per 100.

5. Most older parents don't have serious problems when children leave home. A study by Professor Palmore shows that the "empty nest" syndrome (which has been overrated for all age groups by the media) does not typically have an enduring negative effect.

6. Those under 65 have about 14 accidents per 100 each year while seniors have about half this rate.

7. Seniors are well represented in public office. In the last census, 21 percent of the House of Representatives and 39 percent of the Senate were 60 years or older.

8. The majority of older people don't live alone. In an extensive study, it was found that only 14 percent of the men and 36 percent of the women over 65 lived alone.

SCORE

Consider that 3 to 5 correct answers falls within the average range. The higher you score, the more you know about our older generation. If you score below 3, it's time to become acquainted with some senior citizens in your neighborhood.

DO YOU REHEARSE YOUR ANGER?

W.C. Fields was once asked: "Are clubs good for children?" His tart retort was "Yes, but only if all else fails." Fields' wisecracks, of course, were calculated to maintain his Hollywood image of a rascal of social irreverence not only toward small fry but toward adults as well.

While Fields' hype was done for box office profit, some of us get bogged down with ill-will as a way of life, feeling chilly toward everyone in general and usually losing friends as a result.

But humans are not born mad or hostile rather, frustrations usually cause such emotions to well up within us. If left unchecked they can bring on distorted reactions.

A survey by *Psychology Today* found that those who are grouchy are most likely to be lonely, depressed, and have low self-esteem. So animosity is directly linked with poor emotional well-being.

Many psychotherapists hold that anger is instinctual and they teach clients how to deal with it. But today there is evidence that some notions about anger and its management are inaccurate.

In her book, *Anger, the Misunderstood Emotion*, psychologist Carol Tavris asserts that modern psychology may be doing more harm than good in explaining how to handle angry impulses.

Could all this supposed misinformation be affecting you?

The quiz, based on Tavris's findings, may reveal insights into your notions of anger and how you deal with it. Answer the items True or False then read on.

1. Expressing anger to someone who irritates you is emotionally healthy.

2. Most of the time, men feel angrier than women do.

3. You will reduce your level of anger if you talk things out with a good listener.

4. It's good to blow off steam by engaging in "hostile humor," jokes that contain hostile, aggressive or sarcastic remarks.

5. Noise will almost always make us angry or increase our already existing anger level.

6. Children of angry parents usually grow up to be angry adults.

7. Women usually provoke more anger in others than do men.

8. We are more apt to show anger to strangers than to our loved ones.

9. Women are less likely than men to express anger through physical aggression.

10. A person who is spontaneous in releasing anger is better adjusted than one who is slow to express it.

EXPLANATION

All items are False except item 6, which is true

1. In his book, *The Dynamics of Aggression*, Dr. Jack Hokenson summarizes studies which show that venting anger doesn't always reduce its ill effects. If two people don't, instead, deal with the cause of the anger, it may only worsen.

2. In a national survey of over 2,000 families, reported in the *Psychological Bulletin*, no differences were found between the sexes as far as frequency or level of anger is concerned.

3. Don't count on it. Talking out an emotion may not reduce it. Often it only rehearses and inflames it. One study showed that college students who vented their ire grew more hostile than those who expressed the opposite of their anger or who took neutral positions.

4. It depends on your adrenaline level. Once a person is strongly worked up, hostile humor does not reduce anger. Instead, it tends to increase it.

5. It's not just the decibel level of noise that annoys. People differ in their perceptions of noise. A workman pounding on the house of a neighbor you dislike could be irritating, but the same man hammering on your home is tolerable.

6. This wrongly implies that we inherit our anger patterns. We don't. It's more likely that we learn them from our parents. But it often happens that one may learn new patterns and be more placid to setbacks that would have frustrated our parents.

7. A field study by psychologists W.D. Frost and J.R. Averill, reported in the latter's book, *Anger and Aggression*, shows that men are twice as likely as women to provoke irritation

in others. In general, the people interviewed reported more occasions of anger toward men than toward women.

8. A survey, included in Tavris's book, which summarized 72 studies, concluded that women are just as aggressive as men are but they inflict less physical damage on their targets. However, men are likely to attack strangers more than are women.

9. We show anger more frequently and more intensely to loved ones and to those emotionally close to us than to strangers. This is equally true of both sexes.

10. The reverse is more likely. Quick rage indicates low self-control. A study by M.K. Biaggio, professor of psychology, University of Idaho, found that students quick to express anger were less emotionally healthy than those who showed restraint.

SCORE

Score 1 point for each false answer you gave.

8-10 points. You have a good sense of what will or will not be constructive when dealing with anger.

4-7 points. You have an average understanding of how anger impacts on behavior. There's always room for improvement though.

0-3 points. You have some false notions about anger that probably cause friction with others. Carefully study your style of handling anger. Does it provoke counter-hostility in others? Do you lose friends?

Chances are you'd benefit from more control of this volatile emotion.

Note: On any test, there's always the chance that our precede might clue you in to what the quiz measures and cause you (unwittingly or not) to slant your answers. To see if this is so, ask someone who knows you well to take the quiz with you in mind, and then compare your answers

ARE YOU TURNING OFF YOUR FRIENDS?

When two people meet and hit it off, we say their chemistry is right. In a word, this sums up the very complex process of how people form friendships, still much of a mystery to behavior specialists.

Building a friendship is an acquired skill like writing, reading, speaking, etc. It can be taught as a special art. But even if we learn all the right moves in forming a bond with others, we still may lose friends because of mistaken notions about just what friendship is all about.

To test your notions about friendship, answer true or false to the items ahead. They are based on a national survey by psychologist Joel Block of New York City and summed up in his book, *Friendship: How to Give It and How to Get It*.

1. Our society encourages friendship.
2. The need for friendship decreases with age.

3. Compared with men, women find it harder to count on each other in a crisis.

4. Sexual attraction usually deepens in friendship.

5. Close friendships are more likely to flourish in small towns than in large cities.

6. Despite their fame, celebrities are among the loneliest of people.

7. Both men and women seek similar qualities in friends.

8. Friendship is a free choice and it is not essential for our emotional well being.

EXPLANATION:

All answers are False

Give yourself 1 point for each item you answered false.

1. Although society places a high value on keeping old friends, Block found little evidence that our society encourages new meaningful friendships. We seem to be becoming a fast-moving society of short-term ties and we must accustom ourselves to many temporary friendships and fewer long-term ones.

2. The opposite is more likely. With children grown and careers established, people become less centered on themselves and their families and have more of a need for friendships.

3. This is a popular myth. Women tend to form more emotional attachments with each other than men do and can provide equally strong support to their friends when it is called for.

4. Sexual intimacy often reads "possessiveness," which weakens the bond with a friend. Cross-sex friendships work best when the sexual aspects are low or absent.

5. Small towns don't foster more friends than do cities. A poll of a Midwest community, population 50,000, found that one-third of the working wives had no intimate friends at all and that families tended to spend more time among themselves. The study was repeated a decade later and the findings were verified.

6. Celebs aren't so different from ordinary people. Despite fame and demands on their time, they also need closeness. Interviews show that on average they have as many or as few friends as non-celebrities.

7. Men and women seek different qualities in friends. Women seek openness, compassion and warmth while men look for similarity of interests and activities (golf, tennis, etc., which can be shared).

8. A 1954 mental health study done in midtown Manhattan involving some 1,700 men and women found that friendless people run a higher risk of mental illness compared with those who have friends.

SCORE:

Total your score. To learn what your understanding of friendship is:

7 to 8 points. Above average.

4 to 6 points. Average.

0 to 3 points. Below average.

WHAT ARE YOUR BOGUS NOTIONS ABOUT OTHERS? PART 1

We all "goof" once in a while when it comes to judging others. Many of our errors come from false notions drawn from folklore, myth and rumors. And they often cause conflicts with those around us.

The items below offer you the chance to face your untested assumptions about behavior. Respond True or False to each.

1. We become sadder as we grow older.
2. You can judge someone's personality from a photograph.
3. Fast learners forget more than slow learners.
4. There's a thin line between genius and insanity.
5. In happy marriages, compared to those that are unhappy, partners have sex more often.
6. Venting anger at someone reduces its physical and psychological ill effects on us.
7. Handwriting can reveal one's personality.
8. Unhappy people live just as long as those who are happy.

EXPLANATIONS

All items are false.

1. We don't become sad as we age. A national survey by the National Council on Aging in Washington, D.C., showed that less than one-quarter of those over 65 reported, "This is the dreariest time of my life," while a majority said, "I'm just as happy as when I was younger."

2. Many studies have failed to show that personality traits, as well as mental ability, can be judged from photos. Video pictures do not appreciably increase the accuracy of those judgments either.

3. Fast learners usually have higher intelligence and tend to recall more of what they learn than their slow-learner counterparts.

4. The genius has often been thought of as "different," i.e., mad, unsocial, sickly, etc. This notion has no foundation in fact. One long term study of over 1,300 gifted children conducted by the late professor Lewis Terman of Stanford University showed that they grew up to be superior in many ways: better health, better adjusted socially, better grades, etc. And, when older they also got better jobs.

5. How often couples have sex has more to do with their psychological makeup than their happiness. Some happy couples are content with less sex compared with those who are unhappy. The important thing is that both partners are satisfied with the frequency of their lovemaking.

6. This is a common misunderstanding about anger than isn't always true. Recent investigations by Dr. Leonard Berkowitz of the University of Wisconsin showed that in the process of telling someone off, we frequently stimulate ourselves to continued or even stronger aggression.

7. There is no scientific evidence that one's personality can be analyzed through script. This has been called a "gold brick" psychology because its claims are louder than the hard facts.

8. In the late 1970s, Dr. Erdman Palmore of Duke University devised a "longevity index" to predict the lifespan of people over 65. Using several hundred subjects, he found that those who rated themselves as happy tended to live longer. His index proved to be more accurate than the actuarial tables of insurance companies.

SCORE

Give yourself 1 point for each correct answer. A score of 4 or 5 shows an average degree of insight into behavior and personality. If you scored 3 or less, we suggest a good book or a course in psychology. Chances are it will improve your relationships with others and lead the way to greater self-knowledge, too.

MORE ON YOUR BOGUS NOTIONS ABOUT OTHERS, PART 2

We live in the fastest paced society in history. Alvin Toffler author of *Future Shock* once said that as far as friendships go, ours is a "thrown-away culture." We meet someone, form a short-lasting acquaintance, then we split with them. All too often, because of time pressure perhaps, we make snap judgments about him or her which are based on a furtive glance, a fleeting impression, etc. but later, we're disillusioned.

People reading is the name of the game and if you can size-up someone accurately, you're a winner in human affairs.

Rate your keenness about others by answering the items ahead, true or false:

1. Successful women smile more often than those who are not.
2. Persons prejudiced against one group tend to be prejudiced against other groups as well.
3. A shifty-eyed person is likely to be a liar
4. When a stranger is injured, a bystander is more likely to render aid if he or she is alone than with a group.
5. Older persons generally feel lonelier than those who are younger
6. Infants instinctively fear the dark.
7. People who are good with numbers are usually good with words
8. The last-born in a family tends to have a higher IQ than those born before him.
9. Slow learners remember more than fast learners
10. The blind have a 6th sense which helps them to avoid obstacles.

EXPLANATION

1. False. The opposite is actually true. Social psychologists Wendy McKenna and Florence Denmark of the City University of N.Y. found that women who faced higher status persons showed "low status "gestures like nodding, holding arms in, keeping legs together, and smiling. But women who believed they were of higher status and competence showed a marked decrease of these behaviors, including smiling.

2. True. Prejudice is a trait characteristic like extraversion for example. It therefore has a generalized effect on a person's attitudes and reactions to other targets.

3. False. There is no connection between eye-gaze fixity and honesty. Psychologists Randy Larsen and Todd Shackleford of the University of Michigan found that psychopaths actually maintained steadier eye gaze compared with normals. More likely a shifty eyed person might be shy or introverted.

4. True. Bystanders feel indecisive about assuming responsibility when under group pressure, possibly out of fear of criticism. However they are more willing to help when alone.

5. False. Attitude surveys on elders by the University of California at L.A. and N.Y. University found that they do not feel as lonely as may be commonly believed. Rather the aged tend to be satisfied with their friendships.

6. False. Behavior studies at the Gesell Institute of Yale University confirmed that compared with children or adults, infants have very few fears. They do, however, have three distinct instinctual fear reactions: loud noises, sudden or prolonged stimuli, and loss of physical support.

7. True. Extensive Studies by L.L. Thurstone of Stanford University found that ability with numbers is related to general intelligence which, in turn, is the basis for more word power.

8. False. Test scores of nearly 400,000 adolescents in Holland by Dr. Zick Rubin of Harvard University showed that IQs decrease from the first-born to the last born.

9. False. B.J. Underwood of Northwestern University a leader in learning research reported that slow learners remember less than fast learners for two main reasons: (1) they usually have lower IQs to begin with and have less memory capacity; and, (2) they take longer to learn.

10. False. The blind have no such 6th sense. But classic research at Cornell University confirmed that to some degree, they use their sense of hearing as bats do through a sonar like sensitivity to sound wave frequencies to avoid bumping into things.

WHAT'S YOUR HELPING STYLE?

Did you ever give advice to someone only to find that, in the long run, your efforts didn't make a difference? Don't despair. Even professionals who dispense the wisest of counsel often find themselves in the same boat. As a matter of fact, studies done at the Menninger Foundation in Topeka, Kansas, show that psychotherapists have clear success with only two-thirds of their clients.

It is becoming more apparent that a helper's personality style is an important factor in the outcome of his efforts. Strictly speaking, a lot depends upon the "fit" between the personalities of the helper and the person he helps.

Psychologist Richard Wallen, of the National Training Laboratories Institute, in Washington, D.C., an institution that trains those who deal with human relations problems, has studied the process of how people render aid to others. He concludes that people have characteristic styles of assisting others and no one style is more effective than another. How influential the advice given will be also depends upon the personality of the person seeking help.

Have you ever wondered how others receive your advice? Take the following quiz to learn what your style is. Read the items, grouped together in three clusters and respond "yes" or "no" to each item.

A:

I use friendly, supportive persuasion.

I rely upon a strong dose of trust, affection and consideration.

I try to probe and understand all the feelings and sentiments connected with the problem.

B:

I am very careful to do only what is necessary so the person doesn't become dependent upon me.

I avoid showing sympathy, obvious affection, sadness or distress.

I am effective at giving pep talks and strong words of inspiration to firm up their determination to win.

C:

I remain cool and calm, staying away from emotions and sticking only to the facts.

I rarely make their decision or make a judgment. Instead, I try to present possible solutions, and let them decide.

I try to use reason and logic and sometimes give or recommend reading material on the subject.

ANSWERS

The three clusters correspond to Wallen's three categories of helpers: A. tender helpers; B. tough helpers; and C. logical (or objective) helpers.

If most of your "yes" answers are under cluster A, you are what Wallen would term a warm, friendly helper. Such tender helpers use affection, empathy and lots of assistance to help pull someone out of trouble. This style is most typical of the client-centered therapy that was established by psychologist Dr. Carl Rogers, the director of the Center for the Study of the Human Person, in La Jolla, Calif. Rogers believed that most people possess the power to solve their own problems. He put great emphasis upon caring and understanding to "free up" the healing potential of the distressed person.

If you responded "yes" to most of the items in cluster B, you are a tough-minded helper. Tough-minded helpers are cautious about getting too involved before determining whether the person has brought on his own problem. Helpers with this style are wary of helping too much and creating dependencies that block the development of self-sufficiency.

Tough helpers avoid displaying soft emotions and rely heavily upon strong will and determination in overcoming their own hardships.

Cluster C identifies the logical helpers. They are emotionally detached problem-solvers who are proud of their intelligence and expertise. They emphasize intelligence above all and believe that feelings are more of a hindrance than a help. They usually rely on tried-and-true solutions, and firmly believe there is a rational answer for every problem. They won't do something that the person seeking help can do for himself.

To some degree, most good Samaritans shift their style somewhat depending upon the situation, and can show varying degrees of each.

Before you take on the role of counselor, it is important to match your usually helping style with the personality of your target with the problem. For example, if you are a tender helper, you could easily fail badly when dealing with someone who has responded only to tough authorities all his/her life.

On the other hand, if you are a tough helper, and your target is one who usually seeks out supportive, sympathetic counsel, they may not follow your advice feeling you are too directive.

Extremes usually are not effective in all types of helping situations. If you found that your choice of a cluster was difficult, and that you tend to shift gears equally among all three styles, you are probably flexible and stand the best chance of being an effective helper to a variety of personality types.

ARE YOU INSENSITIVE TO OTHERS?

Everyone has known a "Thelma Thin skin", a fretful type, nervous about how people will size her up. Super-sensitive types who are acutely attuned to what others say and think, are quite guarded in their presence, fearful of perhaps evoking their displeasure.

Our quiz measures IO, interpersonal orientation. This involves one's responsiveness to personal factors of others which might affect them.

Lest we give away the purpose of this test, answer the items True or False, and then read on for answers.

1. Other people are the source of my pleasure and pain.

2. I often talk about my personal life with people I do not know well.

3. I would prefer to flunk an exam which is machine scored than one which is scored by an instructor

4. I wouldn't ever buy something I suspected was stolen

5. Sometimes talking aloud about my worries makes me feel better regardless of whether or not anyone hears my thoughts.

6. I would rather receive a small, simple, thoughtful gift than a more extravagant one which involved less thought and care.

7. The more someone reveals about him or herself the more I am inclined to reveal things about myself.

8. The more I understand a person; the more I tend to like him or her.

9. When people tell me personal things about themselves, I feel closer to them.

10. I am very sensitive to criticism.

11. I can be strongly affected by someone smiling or frowning at me.

12. I am interested in what makes people tick.

13. I am strongly influenced by the moods of those I am with.

14. When I get a gift I usually think of how much it cost.

15. When someone does me a favor I feel compelled to return it.

EXPLANATION

Walter Swap and Jeffery Rubin, psychologists at Tufts University, studied our topic with a sample of over 900 subjects over a 2-year period. Our items are used here, with permission, gauge one's social sensitivity. Some items may appear unrelated at face value to the topic, never the less, they validly show a person's IO score.

A person with a high IO score is very aware of others, too much so. He is interested in and reactive to their behavior and tends to take their judgments personally. He is easily influenced by slights as well as compliments and when rebuffed, may lapse into moodiness. He has more social anxiety than the average. Sometimes, high IO's may not be easy to deal with. They can be so reactive to others that they become choosy in forming friendships.

People with a lower IO trait are less attuned to those around them. They are more concerned with relationships which will promote their personal goals. They are not strongly affected by the actions of others. They are usually drawn to "thing oriented" jobs like engineering, accounting, and science.

SCORE

Take one point for each True answer you gave. Keep in mind, that neither extreme score is desirable.

12-15 points. You have high IO. You are perhaps unduly sensitive to the actions and beliefs of those you meet. The behavior of others affects your morale to a great degree.

6-10 points. You are average and in the desirable range with respect to social sensitivity.

0-5 points. You are low on IO and tend not to focus on the nuances of human interactions. You are relatively unaffected by others in the quest to achieve your own ends. You are probably a competitive, assertive person who has limited social dependency.

"Great news, Bayless! I've worked out the most diabolical fold for a map you ever saw!"

CHAPTER 5
WORK AND CAREER

WOULD YOU BE A RESPECTED BOSS?

It would have been hard not to like a comedian like the late Rodney Dangerfield when he tugged his tight collar and forlornly complained: "I don't get no respect." But even though we are drawn to Dangerfield, his complaints don't earn our respect. In fact there are people who can't have both respect and affection.

In the workplace and in the family too, there are some interesting parallels. Many who assume the role of leader or boss are liked but don't get much respect. Do you recall the teacher, boss or coach who went all out to be nice to everyone, was loved by all, but did not get esteem from his or her subordinates?

And there are also those who are respected but not liked, such as the super efficient boss who gained your high regard for a job well done, but for whom you couldn't feel one iota of warmth.

Being in an authoritarian position, whether on the job or at home, is not easy. You must ensure that those under you perform at maximum capacity and, at the same time, delegate tasks without intimidating your subordinates. It's easy to err in either direction In fact, few people are able to strike a balance between the two extremes.

The following quiz may help you assess your managerial style. If you're a boss or think you could do a good job as a person in charge, take the quiz to find out. Answer true or false to each item then read on for answers.

1. Ambition is essential in leadership.
2. Outdated methods in management must be eliminated in spite of people's feelings.
3. Know-how and initiative are two of the most important qualities a person can have.
4. What gets done is more important than how pleasant it is to perform the task.
5. A supervisor's job is more important than that of a social worker.
6. Newspapers don't give enough space to people who complete worthwhile projects.
7. My primary goal in life is to reach the top of the heap.
8. The greatest satisfaction for me is the feeling of a job well-done.
9. Friends are more important then career ambition.
10. Schools should put less emphasis on competition and more on getting along with others.

EXPLANATION

The goal of any supervisor is to get work done through others, and each manger has his own style of doing so. Harvard University sociologist Robert. F. Bales, has studied this process for more than 25 years. One of his conclusions is that there are two basic types of managers: the task boss, and the social boss. The task boss is sharply focused on the work to be done, the goal to be accomplished. He is the "idea" person who uses others for results. He minimizes the human relation factors in the work setting and strives to get things done as efficiently as possible.

Bales and his associates found that workers see the task boss as a strong leader and one who generates ideas. He tends to give opinions and make more suggestions than his counterpart. He reminds those under him/her of their goals when they stray from their objectives.

At the other extreme is the social boss. He/she is also interested in getting the job done but emphasizes good group relationships. The aim is to create and maintain a good psychological climate in his unit and is responsive to the personal needs of his subordinates.

The social boss (or interactional boss) believes in participatory management. He is likely to ask for suggestions rather than give them. He gives more praise, encouragement and other types of feedback to those under him than does the task boss. What's more, he has more interest and skill in soothing over differences within a group.

SCORE

Many chiefs have traits of both the task and the social boss and your scores may show the same mixture. Taskers would answer true to items 1 through 8 and false to items 9 and 10. Social bosses answer false to items 1 though 8 and true to items 9 and 10.

Take a point for each answer that follows these patterns and consider a score of 3 to 5 in either category as average. Any score above 6 is high and indicates that you would be (or are) either strongly task-oriented or socially-oriented as a boss.

If you are already a manager, you may have found that your own style and your notion of the best supervisory technique conflict. If so, examine the quiz items again and think of ways to change your style.

If you are not a manager, you may be surprised at the way you responded to the items. While on the job, you may often think, "I could do a better job of managing things around here." Now examine your answers to the items. You may be surprised to find that, once given the chance to act as a boss, your ideas about what make an effective manager have changed.

DO YOU HAVE "DECIDOPHOBIA"?

Every moment of our waking life reflects past decisions. With a lifetime of decisions behind us, you might think we are experts at making them. Yet this is rarely the case. For decision making, unlike other learned skills, does not necessarily improve with repetition.

Answer the following items True or False.

1. I tend to repeat New Year's resolutions from year to year.

2. I own many things which I thought I'd use or enjoy but now I regret having bought them.

3. When eating out I am usually the last to select from the menu.

4. I habitually decide to change my personal habits, like fast driving, nail biting, over eating, but don't succeed too well.

5. When confronted with an unpleasant choice, it's best to make a quick decision.

6. I make my decision immediately after I weigh all the facts involved.

7. When faced with a decision, I often become very tense, lose sleep over it, or get a headache or stomach ache.

8. Once all the facts are gathered, I just allow the right solution to come to mind.

ANSWERS

1. True. Decisions requiring continuous commitment are the hardest to fulfill, i.e. eating, drinking, gambling, smoking less. This special class of decisions takes more will power.

2. True. Impulse buying accounts for some 15% of all sales. This "buy now, regret later" syndrome is common among weak decisions makers. Often they buy out of fear that there won't be another chance to get the item. Their choices are based on emotions which dominate them when something delights their fancy.

3. True. People who vacillate between alternatives, more often than not, make poor decisions. Their anxiety is too high to cope with a bad decision, should it happen. After making a choice, its better to stick to it and have a back-up plan should it turn out to be wrong.

4. True. Experiments at Yale University by Irving Janis, author of *A Practical Guide for Making Decisions*, show that here it might be best to use a buddy system. This system has worked well with Alcoholics Anonymous, Weight Watchers, Gamblers Anonymous, and other such groups.

5. True. Hasty decisions usually lead to procrastination. You need more time to let things settle in you mind. Time management consultant Alan Lakein, advises, "Give yourself every opportunity not to ditch the choice rapidly. Slow down the process so that you have time to make a conscious and deliberate choice."

6. True. For some of us it might be upon awakening, while walking, listening to music, or taking a shower. But no matter where or when you come to a decision, you should first take a break. Pioneer mental scientist H. Helmholtz found, and others confirmed, that after you have all the facts you should give your mind a break to digest them. This allows for "incubation" and will help you make the right choice.

7. True. Some of us have experienced such strong criticism over poor judgment, usually as children, that a looming decision becomes a dreaded event. We lapse into *decidophobia* as Dr. Eric. H. Marcus calls it. Recognize that this may also be the case with you. Try to avoid making

decisions when you are angry, tired, ill, or depressed. Sometimes if you wait you may gain new strength and new options. If you know you are a procrastinator, set a deadline and try to keep it.

Often culling more information about the issue can be helpful. Being indecisive doesn't have to be a permanent state of mind. Sometimes we are so swamped by pressing problems and setbacks that we hesitate to make another decision lest we add yet another burden of failure on ourselves.

8. True. There are some techniques you can try to arrive at the right path. One that Benjamin Franklin advised is make a list on paper of all the pros and cons of the issue. Sometimes seeing these in writing can help to weigh all the possible answers.

Also, don't hesitate discussing the question with others who you respect, bearing in mind, however, that you may be dealing with their biases and attitudes.

Poor deciders often don't have insight into themselves. Like Mark Twain, who gave up smoking a thousand times, they often resolve to do something which is noble but unrealistic. The trouble is they don't know themselves well enough to foresee that their vow will fail when the going gets tough.

SCORE

How *decidophobic* are you? Take one point for each matched answer.

7-8 points. You have trouble making sensible decisions. Are you criticized for poor judgment in the things you do? Chances are you have unrealistic expectations about life. You should reflect more before you act for you're probably a 'jiffy decider'.

3-6 points. You're not especially fond of risk taking. You've arrived where you are, by solid effort and consistency. Most of your decisions are on the conservative side but occasionally you like to break out of the mold and wing it on a hunch.

0-2 points. You accept the reality that no choice can be perfect. You are secure enough to take unusual risks to achieve your goals. All in all, you should come out on the winning side in most decisions you make

HOW GOOD A DECISION-MAKER ARE YOU?

When people rhapsodize about their childhood being a time of joy, it might well be because those were the halcyon days when they weren't pressured to decide most serious matters. As grown-ups, it's a different life. Everyday brings with it a flood of decisions to be made.

So how are you faring in the world of choices? Is your mental machinery churning out the best alternatives for you? You could improve your decision-making skills if you know the rights and wrongs of the process?

Answer True or False to each statement below to know.

1. Regardless of their outcome, you can build decision-making skill by attempting as many decisions as possible.

2. There are many different styles of making decisions.

3. When others disagree with us it often hinders us from making successful decisions.

4. For the most part, your life depends pretty much on factors outside of your control.

5. A self-defeating attitude will affect the way you make up your mind.

6. Your emotions should be allowed to freely influence your decisions.

7. When you arrive at a decision, it's a good idea to relax and allow your plan to take form.

8. In a relationship, the decision-maker is always the stronger of the two.

9. The more difficult the decision, the more the likelihood that you will carry it out.

10. After making a hard choice between alternatives, the goal rejected often seems to become more attractive.

ANSWERS

1. False. All decisions should not be yours to make. As a matter of fact, many decisions which turn out wrong could erode your self- confidence and undermine your effectiveness. Ask yourself: Is the choice up to me? Although you may govern some areas of your life, others may be beyond your control.

2. True. You must find ways of deciding that work best for you. In *Decision Making Without Fear*, Dr. Eric Marcus suggests three styles of making choices: passive, impulsive and logical. These styles overlap somewhat but most of us fall into one of these categories.

3. False. Active disagreement by others is an integral part of sound decision-making. Management consultant Peter Drucker in his book *The Effective Executive* asserts that the effective decision maker must organize disagreement. This gives him or her alternatives and protects against being gullible and taken in by the obvious position.

4. False. If this is your attitude then the quality of your decisions will probably suffer. Psychologists John Sims and Duane Baumann found that persons who strongly feel that the control of their lives is mostly up to them, make more accurate and realistic decisions than those who believe their life was up to fate, destiny or luck. This dimension of human experience has been called internal vs. external locus of control.

5. True. Research by Dr. Rolland Parker, author of *Effective Decisions and Emotional Fulfillment*, discloses that a self-destructive attitude often will block your instincts for self-fulfilling choices in life.

6. False. Emotions or "gut feelings" are poor signs to follow making when a judgment. They are usually rooted in our immature wishes. It's true that with nothing else to go on but a hunch, you might follow that lead but when making up your mind be sure that you're not angry, frustrated, sad, etc. Better to calm down and then let your cool reasoning take over.

7. False. A golf swing is only as good as its follow-through and a decision is only as good as your drive and ability to implement it. Making the right decision is only half the battle. The best idea men fail because they don't execute their plan carefully and quickly enough.

8. False. We generally associate decision making with leadership but this isn't always the case. As a matter of fact, the reverse may be true. A spouse or partner may deliberately be

passive to force the other to take charge. Playing helpless or inadequate however, often masks a great deal of power. The person who decides who will make the decisions is usually more dominant. The key question here is: "Who decides who decides?"

9. True. If you've agonized over a decision, say to postpone a vacation to step up payments on a new car, then your motivation to carry through on your plan will be quite strong. Leon Festinger, psychologist and author of *Conflict, Decisions and Dissonance*, found that the stronger the conflict before the decision, the greater the tendency to carry through on the decision afterward. Simply put, if it was a difficult choice, chances are greater that we will stick to it.

10. True. Robert Frost wrote poetically that for each road followed there is one we regret not taking. This 'post-decision regret' is a psychological issue too. Kurt Lewin, the Gestalt therapist, has written that, "after the decision is made, the goal not chosen seems the more attractive one." This Monday morning quarterbacking is common enough in decision-making and it's important to recognize that these feelings don't necessarily mean you've made the wrong choice.

SCORE

8 or more correct. You accept the reality that no choice can be perfect. You are secure enough to take unusual risks to achieve your goals. All in all, you should come out on the winning side in most decisions you make.

4-7 correct. You're not especially fond of risk taking. You've arrived where you are, by solid effort and consistency. Most of your decisions are on the conservative side but occasionally you like to break out of the mold and wing it on a hunch.

3 or fewer correct. You have trouble making sensible decisions. Are you criticized for lower than average judgment about a good many of the things you do? Chances are you have unrealistic expectations about life. You should reflect more before you act for you're probably a 'jiffy decider'.

ARE YOU 'DOING YOUR THING'? (HOW DIFFERENT ARE YOU FROM YOUR PARENTS?)

This has been called the "me" generation, a time when Americans with a debilitating depression and four wars since 1940 behind them, now focus on "doing their own thing." Call it self-fulfillment or self-actualization, if you will, it comes down to getting the most out of your potential and, in the process, reaping the satisfaction that goes with it.

In a survey for his book, *New Rules*, noted sociologist/pollster Daniel Yankelovich found that tens of millions of Americans are now willing to take risks to achieve deeper satisfaction in their lives. Some 73 percent of those sampled feel that they have more freedom of choice about living than their parents did. Their self-confidence is high. About four out of five are certain that they will realize their choices and live the way they "truly want to live."

Yankelovich finds that we have become a nation of strivers. This drive, like all other drives, is strong in some and weak in others. The surveys uncovered certain traits that typify those who are self-formers compared with those who are not. For example, if you're a striver, then you're probably below 35, liberal, single, rent rather than own your residence, and both you and your parents have had some college education.

If you've ever wondered whether you are pursuing life to the fullest extent possible compared with others, the checklist ahead might have the answer.

Mark each item true or false.

1. I spend a good deal of time thinking about myself.

2. I get more satisfaction in achieving my own goals than sharing the triumphs of my family or anyone else.

3. In the present economy, it's important to be well read and educated.

4. Compared with my friends, I feel a stronger need for new and different experiences.

5. People should be totally free to look, dress and live the way they want.

6. I believe my life needs more excitement at this time.

7. I prefer to spend money on traveling than on buying things.

8. I like to seek out new foods and tastes.

9. I avoid junk foods.

10. If I needed it, I would not hesitate to start psychotherapy.

11. If I had a choice, I'd prefer to be more creative rather than to have more money.

12. Bettering myself is important to me and I work very hard at it.

SCORE

Take one point for each True answer and total your score.

9-12 correct. You are one who strongly searches for self-fulfillment. For the most part, you are "in charge of yourself" and are willing to take risks to get the things you want out of life.

5-8 correct. You lead a moderately self-fulfilling life. You follow the traditions of your parents. At the same time, you've adopted some values that are in contrast to theirs.

0-4 correct. You rank low on self-fulfillment. You are comfortable with the status quo. Changes make you uneasy. You'd sacrifice an exciting life for one that was predictable and secure.

Yankelovich found that self-formers (i.e., those who pursue self-fulfillment) are hungry to live their lives to the brim and are "determined to consume every plate on the smorgasbord of human experience." More than their parents did or could, they want to be their own persons and break free of the mold of convention. They are interested in self-expression and in creating opportunities to prove their abilities. They are usually achievement-oriented, work and play hard, and often rise to the top of their companies. They are more aggressive than the average of their peers in getting the things they want out of life.

ARE YOU UNHAPPY AT WORK?

Psychoanalyst Alfred Adler held that emotional health hinges on a harmonious blend of three elements: our love life, social life and work activity. It may be difficult to assess how Americans are doing in the largely private pursuits of love and socializing, but in the arena of work, a barometer exists. Repeated studies tell us that work is not as rewarding an experience as it might be.

One study recently done at Columbia University in New York City shows that the average worker over age 35 changes jobs every three years. Job switches occur because of family moves, career advancement, layoffs, etc. But the most common reason is discontent with the work or the people there. So basically, much of the dissatisfaction concerns unmet personality needs; in other words, a job and worker are often mismatched. As a result, an employee performs poorly and his own needs remain unfulfilled. If any of this sounds familiar, you may have a case of job mismatch.

The following test can help you determine whether you are psychologically suited to your work. Answer each item as follows: 1. Very little or never; 2. Somewhat; 3. Very much.

Compared with earlier times on your job:

1. Do you look forward more than ever to time off?
2. Can you truly say that you enjoy your work?
3. Are you growing increasingly impatient and irritable with others?
4. Do you feel the quality of your job performance is as high as it could be?
5. Do you feel you are earning what you are worth?
6. Do you have self-confidence about your potential?
7. Are you working to improve your job skills?
8. How would you rate your career ambition?
9. Do you have the skills and knowledge needed to work more effectively?
10. Does your company show recognition for your talents by giving you pay hikes, awards, promotions, etc.?

SCORE

Tally your score by adding the numbers that correspond with your answers to each question.

23-30 points. You are well suited to your work and get emotional satisfaction from it. Your job attitudes are constructive and you have an excellent chance for career success.

17-22 points. Your job fitness is on a level equal to that of the average worker. There's room for improvement. Are you doing as much as you can to develop new job skills? Or talking to your supervisor about modifying your responsibilities before deciding to change jobs?

10-16 points. You and you job are probably not well suited to each other. Have you done a serious inventory of your personality and career needs? Ask yourself: What kind of work excites me? What do I do well? What do I do poorly? What gives me pleasure? What types of people would I like to work with? For greater job satisfaction, find the type of work that provides these elements. Perhaps a talk with a career counselor would help.

EXPLANATION

Some years ago, the U.S. Department of Health, Education and Welfare conducted the now famous survey, Work in America. The department found that unhappiness at work is the rule rather than the exception. Men showed more job dissatisfaction than women, and blacks showed more than whites.

These findings were duplicated by investigative reporter Studs Terkel in his book, *Working*. Terkel, who conducted a broad survey of hundreds of workers across the country, concluded: "For many, there is a hardly concealed discontent. The blue-collar blues is no more bitterly sung than the white-collar moan."

Tensions at home and in interpersonal ties often seep into the job situation and, within recent years, corporations have become aware of this and set up employee-assistance programs. Troubled workers are offered personal counseling by specialists outside the company to help overcome anxieties, frustrations and depression, phobias, and problems such as alcoholism and drug abuse.

HEW also found that job satisfaction can result in increased lifespan. Workers who enjoy their jobs not only stay at one job longer, they also live longer. So the importance of on-the-job contentment is not to be taken lightly.

Examine your situation carefully before deciding to take action. Then if you are convinced that your job is unfulfilling, move on to something more gratifying. Sigmund Freud recognized the importance of suitable work when he wrote, "My work at least gives me a secure place in a portion of reality, in the human community." With so much job unrest, if you are suited to your work and enjoy it, you too have found your place in reality and should consider yourself fortunate.

IS YOUR AMBITION LEVEL HIGH ENOUGH?

Front-page pictures of presidential hopefuls are a display of ambition at the very highest level of political life. Power posts demand high success drive. The question arises: Can this trait be measured? Let's see.

In the late 1930's psychiatrist Henry Murray and his colleagues at Harvard University began a series of important long-term studies on people of varying ages and occupations concerning achievement motivation and the desire to succeed. They looked at human ambition in a very interesting and unprecedented way: by analyzing stories that subjects gave about ambiguous drawings of people in various situations. They noted various themes in the stories like isolation, depression, dependency, etc., and could gauge how high a person's achievement level was from the stories. Their work was continued by Harvard psychologist Dr. David McClelland.

A volume of information emerged from this research and the quiz ahead is based on their findings. To estimate how ambitious you are, answer each item as follows:

Disagree 1, Agree 2, Agree strongly 3

1. I like to help my friends when they are in trouble.
2. I am time-conscious about almost anything I do.
3. Luck accounts very little for the success of a substantial number of people.
4. Even though it takes time and energy, I enjoy networking, like rubbing elbows, with others.
5. I enjoy solving different puzzles and problems.
6. True accomplishments in life are more important than having happy times with many friends.
7. I tend to get up early no matter how late I go to bed.
8. I make daily lists of things to do.
9. I like to be neat, organized and always on time.
10. I have more endurance and energy than most of my friends.

SCORE

The items in the quiz are similar to those used in questionnaires that measure achievement motive. People who are highly ambitious tend to answer them as true of themselves. Add up you points and use the following guide to learn what your score means.

24-30 points. You are intensely ambitious. Your drive to succeed can be highly beneficial but keep in mind that a strong drive could also be detrimental. It is important that you relax and enjoy life. Often, people with a high ambition level have a difficult time unwinding. It may be a good idea to speak with a close friend to put your goals in perspective.

16-23 points. You have average achievement needs and can live with limited goals of accomplishment. Your attitude is probably "win some, lose some, but have fun along the way."

10-15 points. Your ambition level is low. Could you be down in the dumps, insecure about your strengths, lacking in aspiration? If you are content with your lot and don't wish to change, that is your choice. If you are dissatisfied, it might be a help to talk it over with a trusted friend or trained career specialist.

EXPLANATION

Murray and McClelland see achievement as a need. It is one of 20 which were extensively probed by them at the Harvard Psychological Clinic. Some others were: the need for dominance, love, nurturance, etc.

Interesting findings emerged from the many studies over the past 60 years. One, for example, is that achievers tend to be loners.

They do not depend upon others to fulfill their needs. Thus, there is a negative tie-in between achievement and social affiliation. High achievers tend to be entrepreneurs. They enjoy being involved in all aspects of a project from the planning through to the finished product. These characteristics show up very early in a person's life and are evident in school, on the playground, at home, etc.

Can children be raised to be ambitious? This is the theme of one of McClelland's best-known books, *The Achieving Society*. He maintains that businessmen with initially low levels of achievement need, who were coached and encouraged, actually were able to raise their levels of aspiration and consequently, expand their business activities to make significant economic contributions to their communities.

Those who strive for success welcome the chance for additional responsibility. This willingness is a sign of self-confidence. Many have a cocky faith in themselves. Lee Iacocca used to quip: "I knew I'd be head of Chrysler because IACOCCA stands for I am chairman of Chrysler Corporation of America."

WILL YOU BE (OR ARE YOU NOW) HAPPY IN RETIREMENT?

Some 80 million Americans are retired, and the number increases yearly. As companies offer early retirement and the IRS extends tax shelters through IRAs and 401K pension plans, more workers than ever are leaving the job market.

But the so-called "golden age" of retirement isn't necessarily a time of joy for all. A survey of 19,000 retirees completed by Temple University, showed that 90 percent were happy living a life away from work. But when questioned closely, most admitted that they would probably be even happier had they planned their retirement more carefully.

What they emphasize is that they should have done better financial planning. But as research by Professor Ross Stagner, formerly of Dartmouth College in Hanover, N.H., and others have found, there is another, more subtle factor that influences adjustment to retirement.

Your notions about yourself and your lifestyle can spell the difference between joy and frustration during retirement. Attitudes about self-esteem, health, social relationships predict adjustment to retirement.

The quiz ahead may help to tell how well you'll adjust to a non-work life (or, if you're already here, how well you have adapted to your lifestyle).

Rate each item, on a scale of 1 to 3 as follows: 1. low; 2. average; 3. high. Then read on to learn what your chances are for a happy retirement.

1. My sense of satisfaction with myself and with the way the world is treating me.

2. My sense of personal worth, my value to others and my confidence about accomplishing worthwhile things in the future.

3. My physical health and energy level.

4. My mental and emotional health, including freedom from worry, guilt, conflict and fear.

5. The strength of my ties with friends, family and loved ones, and my ability to form long-term relationships.

6. My acceptance of being or becoming older and a retired person.

7. My financial status, i.e., monetary assets, and earning power.

8. My involvement with non-vocational activities like hobbies, sports, community or civic affairs.

9. My know-how in choosing capable professionals, i.e. broker, accountant, banker, etc., to handle any of my financial decisions.

10. My ability to avoid wasted actions and to use my time productively when on my own.

EXPLANATION

1. There's a tie in between your sense of overall satisfaction with life now and how well you'll fare in the non-work status.

2. Those who accept retirement maturely usually have a high sense of self-worth.

3. They usually take good care of themselves and have enjoyed good health most of their lives.

4. They are secure and emotionally stable, free from disabling hang-ups.

5. They have developed ties with others and built a lifetime of friendships.

6. They realistically accept growing older and feel capable of accepting worthwhile challenges.

7. They don't get unduly apprehensive or frustrated about money as the years roll on. They began saving and wisely investing before and during their peak earning years.

8. Data from the Social Security Administration and other government departments show that those who make the best adjustment don't wait until age 65 to become interested in productive leisure tasks, hobbies, etc., instead, they develop these throughout their lives.

9. They have enough savvy to pick competent people who can make shrewd decisions about their money management.

10. They don't like to waste their time. They've learned over the years, to use their leisure time in a satisfying and constructive manner.

SCORE

Tally your score. The higher it is, the better your chance for a happy retirement. If you are already retired, your score indicates your overall adjustment to it. If you are not yet retired, the following score categories show how your present habits and attitudes may influence your future happiness.

25-30 points. Your answers are very much like those given by happy retirees who are gratified by their new lifestyle.

17-24 points. You are average as far as your overall outlook on retirement goes and should be able to take the ups and downs that come with a major lifestyle change.

10-16 points. It's possible you are having, or will face some difficulties in retirement. But don't despair; there still may be time to catch up. You can improve your chances of retirement happiness by reviewing each item with an elder counselor and begin to adjust your plans for retirement.

DO YOU SUFFER FROM "LEISURE PHOBIA?"

Maybe this is the time of year when thoughts of vacation begin popping in your mind. A time to get away from the boss, forget the problems of school and home and indulge those fantasies and pent-up longings to escape from the routines of daily living.

But odd as it may sound, some people won't be enjoying their vacations this year. Leisure, plainly, is a threat to them. No matter what they do in their free time, they never really seem to enjoy it. These are the workaholics, the so-called "Sunday neurotics" among us. They conduct their vacations like a business—up at 8, hike by 9, swim by 10... you know the type. They have the "compulsive should" syndrome, which I will explain later. Does this sound like you?

To learn if you will truly relax on this vacation, answer the items as follows:

Not true 1 Somewhat true 2 Very true 3

1. I really don't need as much leisure time as the average person.
2. I am an impatient person.
3. I often speed up to beat a red light.
4. I often look at my watch.
5. I usually thrive on activities which keep me on the go and require my full attention.
6. I usually have difficulty finding interesting things to do in my spare time.
7. I get more fun at my job than I do in recreational activities.
8. I usually get bored sooner than most others on a long train or plane trip.
9. I enjoy working and playing rapidly.
10. I consider myself an assertive person.
11. When I play, I try harder to win than the average person.
12. It bothers me to waste time.

This brief quiz is based on actual case studies of people who become frustrated with unstructured time on their hands. These are the ones who live in the imperative mood. Those who have been swallowed up by the quick tempo of our culture. They must be doing something, anything, just to fill the empty time (and perhaps relieve a sense of guilt). It's what psychoanalyst Karen Horney called "the tyranny of the should" – I should be doing this or I should be doing that. But above all I shouldn't waste time.

EXPLANATION
Total up your points.

A score of 16 or less indicates you are tension free enough to enjoy your vacation. If your score is 17 or more, you have a tendency toward the common malady of our time, "hurry sickness," and probably will struggle to enjoy your free time on this vacation.

But don't despair. There are some things you can do to help insure a pleasant retreat no matter what your score. First, be sure your trip is well planned. Take along what you'll need to offset any periods of boredom or restlessness. Read up on the area you'll visit, i.e., where you'll stay, its attractions, its customs, etc. Be sure there is ample activity to keep you interested. High scorers need places which will have strong appeal for their interests—good food if they are gourmet diners, scenery if they're camera buffs, and plenty of sports if that is their turn-on. Finally, talk with friends or a travel agent about the place you'll visit. They often have upbeat tips that can help you enjoy yourself.

More than anything else, believe that the world will still be there when you return even if others are running the show imperfectly without you.

An old Chinese proverb says: "To be for one day entirely at leisure is to be for one day an immortal." Will you have your day on this vacation?

WHAT'S YOUR "DOLLAR PERSONALITY?"

With all the pressure in our society to gather material goods, it is sometimes tough to be objective about money. Too often, we become its slave rather than its master.

Do you have a sensible perspective on spending and handling money? Could you be using money to attain satisfactions which you can't get through your own abilities?

The quiz ahead may provide the answers. It is based on the work of Herbert Goldberg and Robert Lewis, psychologists at the University of California, and some items are adapted from their book, *Money Madness*.

True or False:

1. I buy things I don't really need or want because they are reasonably priced.

2. I freely spend money on others but am reluctant to spend money on myself.

3. Even when I have enough money, I feel somewhat reluctant (or guilty) about buying necessities for myself such as shoes, a coat, etc.

4. I buy things that are socially "in" and will improve my image.

5. When it comes to buying something strictly for pleasure, i.e., a vacation, a sports watch, show tickets, my first reaction is: I can't afford it, even if I can.

6. If I were shopping for an item worth $45 or more, I would spend a lot of time looking for it.

7. When I make a major purchase such as furniture, a car or major appliance I feel I may be taken advantage of.

8. I insist on paying more of my share of a bill at a bar or restaurant to feel superior, in control or well liked.

9. If I bought an expensive item, I'm likely to tell people what I paid for it even if they don't ask.

10. I usually buy more expensive gifts for my rich friends than I do for those who are worth less wealth-wise.

11. I wouldn't buy something I liked if I thought my friends thought it was cheap.

12. Honestly, I'd feel good if a friend met me shopping in an expensive store.

13. I'd return an item if I thought I could buy it for $8 cheaper in another store.

14. I'd be embarrassed to run into a friend of mine while shopping in a bargain basement in a shabby part of town.

15. I put money aside for the future on a regular basis

EXPLANATION

Money attitudes begin early in life. By age of 4, an average child realizes the connection between money and buying. By age 6, he knows exactly how much each coin is worth. Children also learn through their parents and the media that money is a symbol of prestige. Many of us never outgrow this viewpoint. Just how money and personality are related in normal life circumstances has been given little attention by experts. Psychoanalysts Carl Jung, Sigmund Freud and Alfred Adler did not view money as a positive force, but saw it as a detrimental influence in society which keeps people frustrated and in competition for goods and services.

Because our society is impressed by the rich, the size of our bank account directly colors how we feel about ourselves. Our self-image is directly linked with money and our pride swells when we have it and deflates when we don't.

SCORE

Tally your score by using this key:

1F, 2T, 3T, 4F, 5T, 6T, 7T, 8F, 9F, 10F, 11F, 12F, 13F, 14T, 15T.

13-15 points. You are self-denying when it comes to spending money on yourself. You may be too dependent or too anxious about money for it to be a constructive, healthy force in your life. You would benefit from getting more fun from activities which don't require money, until you learn to be more generous to yourself.

7-12 points. You have moderate attitudes about money. Rather than depend on money to buy happiness; you tend to lean on your own capabilities to accomplish goals and attain fulfillment.

0-6 points. This range depicts a strict perspective about money. You believe that money equals power and prestige, which mean a lot to you. External recognition and regard by others are vital to your feelings of importance and success. You might look down on those whom you think are worth less than you or decline to consider them for friends. You probably should soften your attitudes.

ARE YOU A PROCRASTINATOR?

If you've ever had the urge to drop what you're doing and take a holiday, you're not alone. There's a little bit of the procrastinator in all of us. Dr. Jane B. Burka of the Counseling Center at the University of California (Berkeley), an authority on the subject, says that procrastination is a way of expressing internal conflict about doing something and at the same time, protect a vulnerable sense of self-esteem.

Studies show procrastinators have certain traits in common and the quiz ahead taps these. To find out how much of a "P" person you are, check each item True or False, and then read on.

1. I tend to work harder than my friends do.

2. When given a deadline, I sometimes feel a surge of resistance within me.

3. I tend to be a perfectionist, e.g., I have a need to go over things I do to iron out any flaws.

4. I have sometimes become a bit awed by the prospect of holding down a job (or getting involved in a project) which is a challenge.

5. I often over estimate the time it would take me to complete a job.

6. I have had moments of doubt about my competence in my job skills.

7. I often get into trouble because I forgot to do things which I should do.

8. To do something badly would bother me a great deal.

9. When confronted with a boring or complicated task, I usually exaggerate it into something bigger than it really is.

10. When I face a challenging job I often get the feeling that I'll get in over my head

ANSWERS

Although there is surprisingly little research on procrastination, most scholars dispute the notion that procrastinators are lazy. "It's just the opposite," says Dr. Lenora Yuen, a collaborator on a book with Burka on the subject. "They get a lot done. If you scratch a procrastinator, you'll find a workaholic underneath."(item 1)

Albert Ellis and William Knaus in their book *Overcoming Procrastination*, say that "P" persons are on the increase. They advise people to ask themselves: "So what if I'm not perfect, just get the job done." They have strong fears about failure and disapproval from others. (2, 8)

Procrastination is sometimes seen as resistance to control by others. Often such types have an authority problem in which they don't express opposition directly but show it by getting things done late and beyond the deadline. (3)

Some "P" types feel apprehensive about success and consequently avoid jobs which could lead to it. They are too threatened by the idea of bearing heavy responsibility with no one to turn to if the going gets tough. (4, 7)

It's easy to put off a task if we judge it to be more complex than it really is or if we judge the time required to do it to be far longer than we can afford. (5, 9). This is a trap procrastinators often fall into. Fear of failure often results in putting things off. (10) Such types often have (convenient) memory blocks which blot out the things which they should be doing. (6)

SCORE

For procrastinators, all answers are True. The items correlate highly with the tendency to put things off. Take one point for reach True answer.

If you scored between 3-5, you're about average in the art of putting things off 'til manana.' Scores above 5 indicate a stronger tendency to procrastinate.

TIP

One technique which may help to weaken the habit of putting off doing a task is called chaining. Suppose you've delayed washing the car. Get the process going with a "leading task." This is a very simple step toward the goal and it should be done quickly and easily. It might mean, for example, taking the car out of the garage, or fetching the soap and bucket.

Other examples of a leading task are rolling a sheet of paper into your typewriter or flipping on your computer to lead you to writing that letter or buying a paint brush to lead you to signing up for that art course. A leading task is often just enough momentum to overcome resistance and sustain your motivation to complete a job which has been kept too long on the shelf.

ARE YOU USING YOUR WHOLE BRAIN ON THE JOB?

Are you moving ahead in your job? If your answer is no, knowing which side of your brain is dominant could clue you in to what's impeding your success. In a provocative book, *Whole Brain Thinking* psychologists Jacqueline Wonder and Patricia Donovan explain that the left and right hemispheres of the brain govern different tasks. The right side is the home of intuition, feelings, and inspiration, while the left side is the center of discipline, logic and analysis.

According to the authors, each of us has the potential to use both hemispheres, but one side usually dominates. They call this "brain bias." Their research indicates that it is possible to alert the brain to make it more efficient at work tasks by lateralizing the brain, or developing the opposite side, the side that is seldom used. The positive result of lateralizing is that a person can solve more work problems and assume greater responsibility on the job.

To find out which side of your brain is dominant, take the following quiz, then read on for explanations and exercises that could make you a more successful, valuable employee.

1. I recall faces easily. True or false?
2. Ideas seem to come to me from out of nowhere. True or false?
3. I can understand schematics and diagrams easily. True or false?
4. I like to move furniture and change the decor of my office or home frequently. True or false?
5. I have: a) frequent mood changes; b) almost no mood changes.
6. I like chatting a long while on the phone. True or false?
7. When I read, I strongly visualize the characters, setting and plot of the story. True or false?
8. I prefer working: a) in a group; b) alone.
9. I like social situations that are: a) spontaneous; b) planned in advance.
10. Without looking at my watch, I can pretty well judge what time it is. True or false?

SCORE

Score each answer as follows: All "a" and true answers indicate right-brain dominance. All "b" and "false" answers indicate left-brain dominance. Consider a score of 7 or more in either category to indicate that that side of the brain is dominant. Should you have a close split, such as a score of 5 and 5 or 6 and 4, you are most likely a mixture of the two extremes.

EXPLANATION

Were you surprised to learn which side of your brain is dominant? Perhaps you weren't after reading the explanations of each hemisphere in the introduction. But you may still wonder how this relates to job performance. Left-brain-dominant employees are suited to highly structured jobs, such as accounting, chemistry and computer programming, for these types of jobs call for analysis and sequential skills.

On the other hand, right-brain-dominant workers would probably fare better in fields such as art, writing and athletics, because they are less structured and tap one's creativity and imagination functions centered in the right hemisphere.

Wonder and Donovan have lectured at firms such as Kodak and IBM, and have helped employees boost their skills. For example, Sue Williams, a right-brain-dominant woman, was too empathic while interviewing job candidates. She spent too much time delving into irrelevant anecdotes about their lives, the authors found. She had to learn to control her empathy, get down to business and still leave time for the paperwork after the meeting. She learned to develop better instincts (a left-brain exercise) and thus became more efficient in her job.

On the other hand, Jim Ryan, a left-brain-dominant office manager, was all facts and figures. He was a precise type of person who made heavy demands on his staff. He was admired for this, but at the same time, he was resented because he often overlooked his subordinates' needs for recognition. After "right-brain training" he was able to soften his approach to others and became more aware of their sensitivities.

To improve your job performance, here are some of the authors' recommendations for strengthening the non-dominant side of your brain.

To develop the right side of the brain:

1. Take some risks that you ordinarily might not take, such as going to a horse race, buying a book of chances, trying a new food or taking a new route to work.

2. Relive "aha" experiences: Was it in the shower, or on the way to work that you had that flash of inspiration? Be aware of where and how you experienced it. The more you pay attention, the greater the chance of having other such experiences.

3. Daydream for a few minutes each day. Let your fantasies come and go, and just free-associate ideas and feelings.

To develop the left side of the brain:

1. Organize your closets, your car trunk, and your glove compartment and your files at work. The act of organizing helps to develop the left side of the brain.

2. Analyze: Don't settle for obvious conclusions. At a movie, force yourself to compare the film with others. Match its plot, characters, music, etc. When watching panelists, ask: How are they different? How are they the same?

3. Keep records of most anything that interests you—stock fluctuations, the daily temperature, your car mileage, a team's averages, etc. Increasing your awareness of time and numbers strengthens the left side of the brain.

DOES YOUR JOB BRING OUT THE BEST IN YOU?

Bill Douglas enjoys his new career in sales. As a matter of fact, he regrets having waited so long to change his field, since he never really felt fulfilled in accounting.

Lifelong satisfaction in a job is rare. Some 70 percent of all workers are dissatisfied with their work and would welcome a change. For the remaining contented 30 percent of us, there's a significant reason why we continue in our jobs. It relates to our needs. The fact is we enjoy work that fulfills our deeper needs and our thinking styles. Unfortunately, most of us don't probe our psychodynamics before we choose a job. But, it would be better if we could.

Dr. Alan Rowe, professor of management at the university of Southern Californian has uncovered some crucial factors that relate to happy work adjustment. He identifies four basic human thinking styles. These, if properly matched with our jobs, maximize the chances that we'll be satisfied in those jobs.

If you feel discontent with your position and wonder if a change will help you live up to more of your potential, the quiz below might help. It is based on a test devised by Rowe after some six years of research, and it will suggest whether you and your job are meant for each other.

Read each item ahead and put the number 4 after your first choice and the number 3 after your second choice and 2 for your third choice and 1 for your fourth choice. Use this sample as a guide.

Sample: In my job I look for: a) practical results — 4; b) best solutions — 1; c) new ideas — 2 ; d) good working conditions — 3

1. I enjoy jobs that: a) have much variety– b) involve people– c) allow independent action– d) are technical and defined–

2. My main objective is to: a) be the best in my field– b) feel secure in my job– c) get recognition for my work –d) have a status position

3. When faced with a problem, I: a) apply careful analysis– b) rely on my feelings– c) look for creative paths –d) rely on proven approaches–

4. When uncertain about what to do, I: a) search for facts– b) delay making a decision– c) explore a possible compromise– d) rely on hunches and intuition–

5. Whenever possible I avoid: a) incomplete work– b) conflict with others– c) using numbers or formulas– d) long debates–

6. In social settings I generally: a) think about what is being said– b) listen to conversation– c) observe what is going on– d) speak with others–

7. I am good at remembering: a) places where I met people– b) people's personalities– c) people's faces– d) peoples names–

8. Others consider me: a) disciplined and precise– b) supportive and compassionate– c) imaginative and perfectionist– d) aggressive and domineering–

9. I dislike: a.) boring work– b.) being rejected –c.) following rules– d) losing control of others–

10. I am especially good at: a) solving difficult problems– b) interacting with others– c) seeing many possibilities– d) recalling dates and facts–

SCORE

Now total your score, tallying each letter separately (example: a=35, b=25, c=10, d=30, etc.) and pick the two highest scores. These represent your two major thinking styles, which are defined as follows:

a. Analytical. Analytical people are problem solvers. They have a desire to find the best possible answers. They examine lots of details and use large amounts of data. They are innovative, creative and enjoy variety.

b. Behavioral. Behavioral people need human contacts. They are supportive empathic persons. They use little data in making decisions, preferring to talk things out with others. They communicate easily and prefer to use persuasion instead of pressure to win their point of view.

c. Conceptual. Conceptual persons are broad-minded thinkers who like to contemplate the "big picture." They are future minded and creative.

d. Directive. Directive people are authoritarian taskmasters. They need power and expect results. They are persuasive, act decisively and arc rule and regulation minded. They are highly verbal and tend to rely on intuition.

These patterns predict the kind of work that might suit a person best. Business people, for example, tend to score high on analytical and conceptual. They like to consider many options and develop broad plans for their companies. Technical people, engineers, scientists, etc., are analytical and directive. They enjoy solving problems logically, working with numbers and finding mathematical and scientific answers.

Those in the helping arts, nurses, doctors, social workers, etc., combine conceptual and behavioral frames of mind. They like to work closely with people in developing an understanding of human affairs.

Other combinations are analytical-behavioral, which involves the fields of education and law, and, directive-behavioral, which applies to the fields of sales and politics.

The highest score obtainable in any category is 40, but few persons ever make this. The closer your score is to 40, the stronger your thinking style in that category. Match your thinking style with your present or intended job to find out how compatible you and the job are.

ARE YOU READY FOR A JOB SWITCH?

When Sharon started as an accountant for a blue-chip company four years ago she related that she was eager to succeed. Now she is showing the tell-tale signs of job blahs. She lapses into long fantasies about traveling, being out with friends and generally enjoying herself in a non-work setting.

It's estimated that 40 percent of the work force, like Sharon, are also discontented with their jobs. And it sometimes happens that they don't, or won't, admit to themselves that their jobs or careers no longer hold interest for them.

There is a fair chance that you too may soon be ready for a job or career change. To learn the answer, mark each item ahead true or false, then read on for answers. The items are drawn from research and numerous studies.

1. Within the past six months I find that I am making more work errors than usual.
2. I am rarely sick on my days off, but I have many stress-related illnesses at work.
3. I can't imagine any job-related surprises.
4. I acquired at least three new skills in the past year to make my job easier.
5. People often compliment me for talents which I do not use on my job.
6. Most of the time I am uncomfortable mixing socially with people in my line of work.
7. I am probably paid 25% less than the norm for what I do, but I enjoy job security.
8. I am generally cynical about my job field when approached by newcomers.
9. I spend a lot of time daydreaming about working in another company
10. I must admit I don't like my boss.

EXPLANATION:

Studies by the Department of Health, Education and Welfare show that unhappiness on the job is the rule rather than the exception. And the lower down the company ladder, the more the discontent

Unhappy workers and/or those due for a change fit a specific profile. They tend to be unenthusiastic and careless about their work (item 1). Often they are uncomfortable around eager co-workers (items 6 and 8). They just maintain minimum competence to keep their jobs (items 4&5). They are content with trading less salary for job security (item 7). They no longer see their jobs as exciting and they often function with much inner tension (items 2 and 3). They can do their jobs in their sleep and often do. They get continual thoughts about other jobs (9). They often dislike many of their fellow workers, including their superiors (10).

SCORE:

Give yourself one point for each true answer, except item 4, which is false.

0-3 points. You are well matched with your work and receive satisfaction from it. You have a good chance of career success.

4-8 points. Your job fitness is average. There is probably some room for improvement, however. Are you doing all you can to develop new job skills to move up in your career?

9 or more points. You and your work are probably not suited to each other. Have you studied your personality and its career needs? Ask yourself, what kind of work excites me? What do I do well or poorly? Perhaps a talk with a career counselor is in order.

"How are things otherwise?"

CHAPTER 6

DO YOU HAVE WHAT IT TAKES TO BE A SUCCESS?

WHAT'S SO FUNNY? (HOW'S YOUR SENSE OF HUMOR?)

If you have it you're popular, if you don't you're avoided. We're talking about a sense of humor–that distinct human quality which generates good feeling tone with others, keeps us sound in mind and body, and generally gives us the perspective which makes life easier to bear.

To see humor in life seems to be an innate capacity. Strictly speaking, even the highest level of animals (the apes) doesn't have it. Infants usually smile in response to a smile by as early as 60 days and outright laughter appears about a month later.

It's estimated that the average person laughs 15 times a day and women do it more than men do. But reactions to humor are highly variable and complex. Regarding specific jokes, what to some people is dull, to others, is hilarious, depending upon their mind set at the time.

Our quiz gauges sense of humor. To learn where you stand on this desirable trait of young and old alike, take it, and then read on for answers.

PART I

Rate yourself on these 4 items as follows: (1) not true (2) slightly true (3) true for the most part (4) very true.

I consider myself:

1. a fun-loving person
2. socially assertive
3. good at remembering jokes
4. above average in sex drive

PART II

Now pick what you consider to be the funnier joke in each pair ahead:

5. A. The prisoner standing before the firing squad is asked by the officer if he wants to smoke a last cigarette. "No thanks," he answers. "I'm trying to give them up."

   B. Which animals can jump higher than a tree? "All animals. Trees can't jump."

6. A. "If you don't stop playing that horn, I'll go crazy". Other person: "Too late! I stopped an hour ago."

B. Foreman: "Hey you. How come you're only carrying one box while the others are hauling two?"

Longshoreman: "Hell man, I guess they're just too lazy to make two trips like I do."

7. A. "Tell me how long cows should be milked?" Answer: "They should be milked the same as short ones."

B. Mother: "Do you know what happens to little boys who tell lies?" Son: "Yes Mom. They travel for half fare."

8. A. A motorist who ran over a small dog tried to console its owner by saying: "I'll be happy to replace your pet, madam." The reply took only a second: "Sir, don't flatter yourself."

B. After an astronomy lecture, an elderly matron asked nervously, "How long did you say it would take for the sun to burn out?" Answer: "Oh, about 5 billion years". Matron: "Whew, I thought you said million."

9. A. There's the story of the woman who joined a computer dating service asking for a sociable man, who enjoys water sports, going out formally and is on the short side...and they sent her a penguin.

B. A young, nervous doctor shakily fills out his first death certificate and signs his name under the heading "Cause of Death."

10. A. If you must borrow money, pick on a pessimist; he doesn't expect to be paid back.

B. My wife is so clean she puts newspapers under the coo coo clock.

EXPLANATION

There is no one satisfactory theory of humor today. Science is just about where it was centuries ago when philosophers tried to explain the trait.

Sigmund Freud, though now much criticized for his psychoanalytic theories, was the first to write a scholarly book, still highly regarded, on the subject. He saw man's wit as a mature attempt to cope with his suffering, a kind of momentary denial of the hard facts of life, which helps us to revitalize us and carry on. He concluded that humor serves two purposes: (1) it is a mature device used to lessen one's frustrations and (2) it is a release of pent up or repressed drives and emotions.

SCORE

Part I. The first 4 items in our quiz are traits which are associated with a high sense of humor. Total up your ratings for Part I.

Part II. Items 5 to 10 consist of jokes rated high or low on funniness by a panel of psychologist judges (a common method for rating humor and wit).

Give yourself 2 points for all A answers and 1 point for all B answers. Now, add up your points from parts I and II to obtain your total score. Consider the following as a rough estimate of your sense of humor:

28-34 points. Keen as **DAVID LETTERMAN.**

14-27 points. Average as anyone else.

0-13 points. Move over, Count Dracula.

DO SEXY JOKES FROST OLDER FOLKS? (WHAT'S YOUR HUMOR IQ?)

Young or old, humor is a reaction that delights us all. But serious study of just what could tickle our funny bone is a complicated topic. As a matter of fact, just why we laugh at all is a mystery to behavior scientists.

If you're having fun, then abruptly decide to dissect the anatomy of a joke, don't! Be warned that if you do, it will surely take all the joy out of it. Better to accept your titters as a rare human gift (like art) to be enjoyed without too much thought and let it go at that.

On the other hand, if you were serious about it as a subject of investigation, humor could be a fascinating topic.

Although you may pride yourself on having a good sense of humor how much do you really know about it? Did you know, for example that women tend to smile and laugh more than men do?

This quiz tests your knowledge of wit, wisdom and the world of funniness. Answer each item true or false, explanations follow.

1. The more intelligent you are, the more you will appreciate wit.

2. Because it is spontaneous and unrehearsed most of the time, a laugh is a pretty true indicator of how we feel.

3. Possibly because of their preoccupation with inner thoughts, creative people tend to have a lower sense of humor than those who are not creative.

4. Smiling in response to another's smile doesn't occur in a baby until the age of 4 months or later.

5. Although the average person may smile often, he laughs only a few times each day.

6. Contrary to popular belief, men and women appreciate hostile wit equally.

7. Humor is a learned human response found only in civilized societies.

8. If a person became emotionally disturbed, one of the last faculties to be adversely affected would be sense of humor.

9. Sexual humor is enjoyed equally well by both men and women.

10. Men appreciate nonsense wit more than women do.

11. Of the following, which is the most popular: a) hostile jokes; b) sexual jokes; c) ethnic jokes.

12. Men appreciate comediennes more than women do.

SCORE & EXPLANATION

1. True. Wit and IQ are related. But even those with low IQs have a sense of humor, though its range is narrow and its level low. Whether we initiate or respond to jest depends upon our flexibility to perceive things as funny. So, humor is more a personality trait rather than just related to IQ.

2. False. We can't be certain that one who laughs is not inwardly feeling some other emotion. Freud felt that anger was often behind laughter. He argued that our reaction to jokes often allows us to vent pent-up feelings but in disguised form.

3. False. Creative persons tend to be freer and less rigidly controlled and this contributes to their above-average sense of humor.

4. False. A baby comprehends a smile and imitates it by the second month of age. Laughter appears about a month later.

5. False. The average person laughs about 15 times each day.

6. False. Men respond to hostile wit more than women do.

7. False. Humor is an unlearned human reaction found in the most primitive of societies. Some higher animals also seem to engage in mirth occasionally.

8. False. One's humor is one of the first responses to be affected by emotional stress. Tests of humor appreciation sometimes are used to screen those who are mentally disturbed.

9. False. A humor survey by *Psychology Today* magazine found that young or old, both sexes enjoy sexual jokes, but men exceed women in their appreciation of this type of humor.

10. False. The survey, which queried some 14,000 readers, found that women enjoy nonsense wit more than men do.

11. Answer b). Sexual jokes are popular because people get satisfaction out of openly discussing a taboo subject. Often jokes relieve an individual's anxiety about a subject.

12. False. Both sexes prefer a male comic to entertain them, but women like comedieanns better than men do.

Give yourself one point for each correct answer. If you score 6 or more you're average or better on the subject.

DO YOU HAVE TRAITS OF A CREATIVE PERSON?

After months of failure searching for natural rubber in plants, a discouraged assistant to Thomas Edison lamented, "Mr. Edison, we've done 50,000 experiments and haven't had any good results." Edison replied with enthusiasm, "Results. We have wonderful results. We now know of 50,000 things which won't work."

The dialogue points out that one of the virtues of the creative mind is its readiness for wit. But, as we shall see, this isn't the only trait which identified a creative person.

The scientist most prominent in identifying traits of creativity was J. P. Guilford, professor emeritus of the University of Southern California. He directed a major study (the Aptitude Research Project) that lasted several years and yielded many important facts about human creativity. After a lifetime of work, he concluded that creative types have several personality traits in common.

The following quiz reflects these behavioral patterns.

Answer true or false to each item to find out if you are creative or have the potential to be.

1. I was closer to my mother than to my father.
2. I have always been a good reader.
3. I usually daydream more than most of my friends do.
4. I believe my intelligence is not high enough to be imaginative and creative.
5. Since our IQs are limited we cannot increase our problem solving.
6. It is always easier to solve a problem if you are eager to do so.
7. It's best to strongly focus all your attention on your problem and try to think it through.
8. It's best to be under some degree of stress when trying to solve a problem.
9. Repeated success will always increase our ability to be a good problem solver.
10. To be creative we must apply consistent effort to our difficulty.

ANSWERS AND EXPLANATIONS

To calculate your score, read the answers and explanations below and take 1 point for each correct answer.

1. True. Studies by psychologists J. Singer and R. Schonbar of Yale University show that for some reason, those who identify with their mother tend to be more creative thinkers than those who identify with their father. By the way, the researchers did not find the mothers to be more creative problem solvers than fathers, necessarily.

2. True. A study of over 500 suburban schoolchildren in Philadelphia showed that reading skill and creative thinking ability go together. If you were a good reader as a child, you stand a better chance of being an inventive person than if you were a poor reader.

3. True. The psychologists at Yale also learned that daydreaming and creative thinking are correlated. One who is free to daydream is also free enough to allow his imagination to move creatively toward the solution of a dilemma.

4. False. There is no connection between IQ and creative thinking. Creativity exists on different levels. Even a person of low-average IQ can be an idea man within his own limits. By the same token, a very bright person may fail to be creative in his day-to-day living.

5. False. Productive thinking can be taught. Scientists M. Covington and R. Crutchfield of the University of California at Berkeley developed a program of imaginative thinking using games, puzzles, exercises and lessons that proved to be highly successful for thousands of school children. They concluded: "The basic idea is to teach them to use their minds in the manner of imaginative scientists, scholars and detectives."

6. False. Although we should have some degree of interest in a problem, if our intensity of motivation is too high it can hamper us. As our enthusiasm increases, our effectiveness may

also increase but only to an optimal point. Beyond that point, our eagerness will be a deterrent to our efficiency.

7. False. It is virtually impossible to force our minds to yield an answer to a troubling question. The European psychoanalyst, Viktor Frankl, discovered what he called "paradoxical intention." This means we should divert our attention away from our problem, take a break and forget it awhile. Later, when we return to the puzzle, we will see other aspects of it that weren't noticed before.

8. True. It may appear wise to relax and just allow the solution to surface in you but in actuality, this is not so. A small degree of pressure on us energizes our nervous system enough to produce better quality thinking and memory, as well.

9. False. There is such a thing as being overconfident. When we amass a large number of successes behind us we might form a "functional fixity" which means we become complacent and uncreative and apply old solutions to new problems. It is here that we fail.

10. False. The solution to an enigma may often be available at an unconscious level, although we seldom tap this resource. When we sleep on a problem we allow our mind to dwell on it. If practical, let a few days go by before you make an important decision. This incubation period may produce a creative solution.

SCORE

0-2 points. You are not at your best as a creative person. You would function best when you follow a set plan of action.

3-6 points. You are among the majority of us who have average creative power.

7-10 points. You are a creative thinker. You should be involved in something which offers you the chance to be an "idea person."

COULD YOU BE A BREAKTHROUGH THINKER?

It was J.P. Guilford, professor emeritus of the University of Southern California, who was the most prominent in identifying creativity traits. After a lifetime of work, he concluded that creative persons have several traits in common. They tend to think and act in certain ways compared with others and the quiz ahead reflects these behavioral patterns.

To find if you are creative or have the potential for breakthrough thinking, answer True or False to the statements.

1. I like to be engaged in several projects at the same time.
2. I crack jokes, laugh a lot and generally see humor in the things I do.
3. When something new is presented to me, I generally become quite enthusiastic.
4. I consider myself more sensitive (thin-skinned) than my friends.
5. I am resourceful when it comes to the unexpected, i.e., the sudden arrival of guests, a change in trip plans, or a spontaneous picnic.
6. I get a lot of satisfaction out of doing unconventional things.

7. I have a wide range of interests such as the arts, outdoor sports, books, and crafts.

8. I have more energy than most of my friends have.

9. Compared with the average person, I sometimes break certain rules and do things I am not supposed to do.

10. I enjoy experimenting even if the result is unsatisfactory.

11. I value my own self-respect more than I do the respect of others.

12. I think it is proper to dress according to current trends.

EXPLANATION

In a nutshell, creative people display a good sense of humor, enjoy having several irons in the fire and are usually enthusiastic about novelty (items 1, 2, 3). They are quite adaptable to quick changes, new settings and somewhat sensitive to rebuffs (4, 5, 11). They pursue a wide range of interests at a fast pace and are among the non-conformists of the community (6, 7, 8, 9, 10, 12).

Being creative has to do with the ability to overcome what psychologists call a "constraining mental set"—that is, having the flexibility to diverge from conventional ways of looking at things. People who are such "breakaway" thinkers are the ones who compose songs, write novels and plays, and invent devices that make life easier and more enjoyable.

Innovative thinking exists in degrees in everything we do, not only in art, science and business, but also in everyday affairs like interior decorating, story-telling and constructive problem-solving in human affairs. A mother who succeeds in getting her child to eat vegetables by offering a novel reward is being creative.

Not many of us can look forward to being creative geniuses, but we can be encouraged to use our imagination more, thus bringing originality to the things we do. You can be more imaginative by just telling yourself to be so and then, really trying to be just that.

SCORE

Score a point for each True answer you gave.

10-12 points. Creative persons tend to say True to the items, as you have done. You would be happy in activities that call for this ability.

5-9 points. You have average creative power. Try to push yourself to use it more in the things you do and you can boost your creativity.

0-4 points. You are below average on creativity and may need stimulation. Perhaps being in an artistic class or joining an activity group will stretch your creative capacity. Remember, people in fields like advertising, public relations, and commercial art, train themselves for "creativity on demand," and succeed even when the stress is put on them.

BEDTIME STORIES: CAN DREAMS REVEAL YOUR HIDDEN CREATIVITY?

Would you ever think that your attitudes about dreams could tell how creative you are? Research shows that creative persons, even though some of their notions may be inaccurate, place more emphasis on the value of dreams to understand their conscious life than do non-creative types. That is, they are more "in contact" with their inner world (imagination, feelings, emotions, and dreams) than are non-creative persons.

Dr. George Domino, professor of psychology at the University of Arizona, administered a dream attitudes questionnaire to both highly creative and non-creative persons. Sharp differences were found between the two groups. The results showed that the way one feels about dreams offers a gauge of creative ability.

The following quiz, printed here with permission, is based on the work of Domino as it appeared in *The Journal of Creative Behavior*.

Answer each item true or false, then read on to find out if your answers correspond with those given by creative people.

1. Dreams often predict the future.
2. Dreams usually have hidden meanings.
3. Dreams often reveal the goals I wish to achieve.
4. Understanding one's dreams can improve one's life.
5. I often make a special effort to recall my dreams.
6. Dreams are like a window to the unconscious mind.
7. Before sleeping it is possible to direct yourself to dream about a certain subject.
8. Everyone dreams every night.
9. Remembering dreams is a sign of good imagination.
10. Dreams are full of symbols.

ANSWERS AND EXPLANATIONS

Creative persons tend to answer true to all questions regardless of whether they are scientifically true or false. Here's the rundown:

1. It is debatable whether dreams predict the future. Although some cases have been documented, we have no overwhelming proof that dreams can foretell what's ahead.

2. All dreams have hidden meanings, but the problem is we don't yet know how to determine them accurately.

3. This is more likely to be true than false. Dreams are an extension of our conscious life. Therefore it's probable that what we think about when awake such as goals, wishes, fears, etc., will carry over to our dreams. Creative people believe this is true of them more than non-creative persons do.

4. Creative individuals, in general, strongly believe this and it is probably true. Again, it may be difficult to know just what dreams do indicate.

5. Creatives work harder at recalling their dreams than non-creative people do.

6. Creative types firmly believe, along with the experts, that dreams are a road to the unconscious. They make more of an effort to figure out the unconscious meanings of their dreams.

7. There is some evidence that people can program their dreams if they give themselves a suggestion before retiring. Creative people are usually better at this than those who are non-creative.

8. It is true that everyone dreams nightly, but they may not recall their dreams the next morning.

9. Although creative persons believe this is so, studies show that it is not necessarily the case. Some people may be highly imaginative yet have little recall of their dreams.

10. Creative types don't take dreams at face value. They conclude, and rightly so, that dreams are highly symbolic, distorted and condensed versions of reality.

Take 1 point for each true answer
SCORE
7-10 PTS-YOU ARE HIGH ON CREATIVE POTENTIAL
3-6 PTS-YOU ARE AVERAGE ON CREATIVE POTENTIAL
0-2 PTS-YOU ARE LOW ON CREATIVE POTENTIAL

Attitudes about the meaning of dreams vary widely. The basis for interpretations of dreams could be religious, metaphysical, superstitious, or attributable to just a digestive murmur of something we ate. Domino concludes that creative types take their dreams seriously and use them as a potential reservoir from which to draw inspiration. Hence, they are motivated to pay more attention to their dreams and leave themselves open to inner psychic cues.

Here are some other signals that tell if you are prone to being a creative person. You dream more often in color than in black and white, sleep soundly, have solved a problem or overcome a challenge through a dream you had, usually take 20 minutes or less to fall asleep.

ARE YOU AN UNDISCOVERED LEADER?

What do Barack Obama, oil tycoon T. Boone Pickens and the Dali Lama have in common? As varied a trio as they might seem, they all play a leadership role in their day-to-day living.

You probably don't have or would not want, the responsibilities of these giants of influence, but on a lesser scale, whether a volunteer at church, a company worker or a salesperson, have you ever wondered if you could do a better job than those who supervise you?

It's a perfectly normal fantasy and thousands of "you-can-do-it" books are written each year to coax you out of your reticence. And perhaps you just might assume the banner of leadership after you take the quiz ahead. It is culled from years of research and it might help you decide if you will handle this year's community fund drive, be coach of the ball team or supervise your work unit. Answer each item True or False, to learn if you have hidden leadership potential.

1. I believe that true leaders are born with a capacity for leadership.
2. I sometimes disagree with my supervisors and prove them wrong.
3. I have always been good at selling.
4. If I led a group I would probably keep a "low profile" yet manage them closely from afar.

5. In directing others, it would be important for me to maintain a forceful personality

6. It would be important for me, as a chief, to make quick decisions.

7. If I were in charge at work, I would improve output by increasing salaries.

8. It would be weak of me to back down from a decision even if it were unpopular with those under me.

EXPLANATION AND ANSWERS

1. False. Talent to direct others isn't inherited. It's important to have faith in the fact that it's an ability which you can learn, much the same as you learned reading and math. Companies spend millions of dollars developing managers through leadership training programs.

2. False. Those with leadership potential occasionally show some "healthy" difference of opinion with those at the top but they don't often create waves in doing so. Essentially, they are in agreement and harmony with peers and bosses. The comers in a company are not the radicals who are highly non-conforming with those around them.

3. True. Good leaders must be capable of selling ideas and influencing others to try them. At the same time, they must be able to rally their troops to implement a project.

4. False. Effective managers are seen. They keep in contact with those under them. Studies by Professor Richard Lester of Maxwell Air Force Base, Ala., showed that the best leaders have high visibility. They are always on the scene, leaving footprints as they go. You can't be a lone wolf and expect to lead the pack.

5. False. Compared with intelligence and persuasiveness, dominance is a minor quality. Research at the University of California found that one essential of good leadership is the skill to influence others through straight talk and no-nonsense communication.

6. False. If the people you try to lead are faster thinkers than you are, don't let it ruffle you. Studies at Ohio State University showed that a quick mind is much less important than good judgment and ability to evaluate all facts carefully before taking action.

7. False. Money as a work incentive isn't as crucial as generally believed, unless, of course, it is a great amount. Dr. Frederick Herzberg of Case Western Reserve University found that giving personal recognition is, by far, the most powerful motivator. It increases as a motivator the higher up the work scale you go. Give more praise and pats on the back and it will surprise you how much it will help you to be a better leader.

8. False. Being rigid won't gain you supporters. A good head tries to hear all arguments if he/she expects others to pursue a goal. When possible, he uses a democratic process, even if it be slower and more tedious, to uncover disagreements until a compromise is reached. He knows that workers tend to defend that which they create.

SCORE

Give yourself a point for each correct answer. A score of 4-6 correct answers is average. The higher you score, the more likely you will be an effective leader.

TRAITS OF LEADERS

The research shows these traits to be most common in leaders: Pleasing appearance, tallness, self-confidence, sociability, determination, energy level, and good intelligence.

Leaders usually devote time and energy to volunteer work in church, school and community groups.

HOW SELF-CONFIDENT ARE YOU?

Self-confidence is a faith in our ability to accomplish something. It starts early with actions like grasping and touching, then builds gradually through successful experiences. Later, it is bolstered by skills in solving complex life problems.

But it's not a perfect learning path for all of us. Where do you stand? If you've never gauged your self- confidence, our quiz might provide that chance. The items are similar to those found on numerous personality questionnaires that measure emotional growth.

Use this 3-point scale to indicate how true each statement is of you: 1.Very true. 2. Somewhat true. 3. False.

1. I spend a lot of time checking and rechecking the things I complete.
2. I get self-critical thoughts.
3. I don't feel a sense of achievement in things I do, e.g., work, hobbies, sports, etc.
4. I don't enjoy the challenge of "selling" an idea to someone.
5. I don't boast about my accomplishments.
6. When attempting something new, I have a fear of failing at it.
7. Down deep, I don't like it when the joke's on me.
8. I get excellent thoughts to express to others, but only after we've parted.
9. Large crowds confuse or frighten me.
10. I often have unpleasant dreams in which I am helpless.
11. Down deep I feel that my parents didn't really love me very much.
12. I have frequently wished that I could act more spontaneously when with friends.

EXPLANATION:

Self-confidence doesn't stand alone. It is part of a cluster of traits that depicts a healthy and productive individual. Professor Harrison Gough of the University of California at Los Angeles found that people with high self-confidence tend to be extroverts who are dominant socially and are good at problem solving. They tend to answer the items as untrue of themselves. Gough's studies provide the following answers for the statements:

1. Those with low self-confidence (low SC types) often have doubts about their abilities to do a job correctly.
2. Self-criticism and self- confidence usually don't go together.

3. More often than not, those with high self-confidence feel achievement in the things they do.

4. "Selling" an idea, for a high SC type, is usually seen as a chance to turn a challenge into another success.

5. Those who are self-confident are normally proud to tell about their victories to others.

6. Those with shaky self-confidence live with the dread of social rejection should they fail at something.

7. Self confidence goes with self-acceptance. The ability to laugh at yourself is one of the strong signs of both these traits.

8. Those with self-confidence are not shy about speaking their mind to others. Some may even be brash about it.

9. Crowds suggest multiple challenges to interact with others, which is a threat to low self-confidence people.

10. Personal insecurity often appears in dreams as helplessness.

11. This is often reported by low SC types.

12. Low SC types inhibit their free flowing spontaneity.

SCORE

Total up your points and consider that:

30-36 points. You are a winner who has high self-confidence.

20-29 points. You are average on self-confidence.

12-19 points. You are low on self-confidence.

Read carefully through the items and try to improve on the behavior mentioned there.

IMPORTANT NOTE

Self-confidence is situational not absolute. It is always relative to the task and situation. Mary might be confident in Math but lack confidence in English. She may also lack confidence in meeting people.

Although self-confidence is primarily situational, it may generalize across many situations. Suppose Mary was good not only in Math but in almost all academic subjects. She would probably develop self-confidence for learning any academic subject, even those she had not attempted.

If she were also good at sports, people skills, and other life areas, then she would probably develop a high level of self-confidence in general.

COULD YOU BECOME A CON ARTIST?

It was psychoanalyst Dr. Alfred Adler who originated the term inferiority complex. He declared that man's primary drive is to gain power over others. Studies verify that those who rise to the top in most societies have one trait that distinguishes them from others, namely, a strong talent for directing the thinking and actions of others. These are the high-achievers in all walks of life who successfully exert influence on others. But, as we shall see, there are ways of doing this that are frowned upon by society.

Psychologists Charles Turner, Daniel Martinez and Richard Christie of Columbia University independently probed personal characteristics that mark a person for success either socially or on the job. Several traits turned up such as IQ, education level, school achievement, social background and the personality of one's parents. But the investigators learned that it isn't only these traits that predict who ascends the socioeconomic pyramid. As a matter of fact, the above traits account for only 65 percent, at most, of one's occupational attainment and income level.

Notwithstanding a little bit of luck to boost one up, the other 35 percent is attributable to a personality factor loosely defined as a skill in getting others to do what you want.

Whether you are at the top of your success ladder, struggling midway, or angling for a toehold on that first rung, the following quiz might reveal whether you rely unwittingly or not on this special trait to get ahead. We won't give more information about the purpose of our quiz lest we tip you off to its true purpose and perhaps bias your answers.

Note: We grant that no statement can cover all possible variations of a situation, but indicate whether, for the most part, you think the item is true or false. Be honest!

1. It is best to tell a white lie to avoid hassles.

2. It is probably shrewd to flatter important people who are in a position to help you.

3. All in all, it is better to be humble and honest than important and somewhat dishonest.

4. In this strongly competitive world, most anything short of being unethical is justified in getting ahead.

5. Most successful people lead clean, honest lives.

6. P.T. Barnum was right when he said there's a sucker born every minute.

7. It is not possible to abide by all the rules and get ahead in this world.

8. Most people are brave.

9. The biggest difference between law violators and others is that the violators were not smart enough to avoid being caught.

10. Don't tell anyone the real reason for doing something unless it is useful to do so.

The quiz is adapted from the work of professors Turner and Martinez, which appeared in the Journal of Sociometry.

Answer Key. 1. T; 2. T; 3. F; 4. T; 5. F; 6. T; 7. T; 8. F; 9. T; 10. T.

Give yourself 1 point for each correct answer given in the key.

EXPLANATION

For want of a better term, the quiz measures manipulativeness or Machiavellian tendencies. Such tactics in military, government and business affairs derived from Niccolo Machiavelli, an influential political writer of the 15th century. As counsel to royalty, he advocated the use of cunning and contrivance when needed to assure one's political goals. Compared to his other ideas, these amoral aspects of his doctrines have always attracted the greatest attention, yet he devised brilliant strategies to make Italy a free republic. Nonetheless, his name is equated with power and manipulation.

You don't have to be smart to be Machiavellian. These manipulative tendencies do not correlate with IQs, as many might believe. Both bright and dull people can be high Mach types, the difference being that the bright high Machs are most likely to succeed while those less crafty can't conceal their motives as readily.

Also it is not true that con artist power drives go hand in hand with psychopathology; many normal persons use power tactics because these work for them sometimes.

Manipulativeness is probably learned from our parents. This is confirmed by Dr. F. Geis and Richard Christie in their book, *Studies in Machiavellianism*. Although Machs are found between both sexes, studies show that men are more manipulative than women. An interesting finding is that in homes where parents are high Machs, the child who escapes this influence is likely to be the first born who often develops traits diametrically opposite to the tactics of his/her canny parents.

SCORE

3 or fewer points. You are a low Mach person and tend to be more than willing to entertain another person's viewpoint. You are a harmonizer and, at times, may even be a little too submissive in carrying through on your own ideas and goals.

4-6 points. You are average when it comes to conning others. You are likely to push your ideas moderately but not to the point of overruling or manipulating others.

7 or more points. You are a high Mach. You do not share traditional notions about social right and wrong. You are an independent thinker who dislikes conforming to your peers. According to the researchers at Columbia, you are cool and at times, even distant. You might sometimes treat others as objects. If this is you, it might be time to develop more empathy for others.

SPOTTING A MANIPULATOR

High Machs (con artists) tend to be credible, attractive and with an action-oriented message. Their easiest target is a suggestible person with low IQ, especially if he/she has low self-esteem. They succeed when their prey is distracted or indecisive.

Body language experts tell us not to look for shifty eyes as a sign of insincerity. Film studies show that individuals with heavy experience at deception actually have a steadier eye gaze than those who are honest.

WHAT YOUR BODY LANGUAGE REVEALS TO OTHERS

Professor Allan Mazur of Syracuse University, who has studied body language for many years, states that confidence, insecurity, even respect or disrespect are revealed by the way you move your body. These actions can influence others almost as much as our words. Mazur's subject, called kinesis, the study of body movements, began in earnest by psychologists back in the 1930s.

How aware are you of what our body actions tell about us? Mark the items ahead true or false, then read on for explanations.

1. A steady unwavering eye gaze indicates that a person is telling us the truth.

2. A cold and clammy handshake shows that a person is nervous and insecure.

3. If a person shows quick, almost automatic movements when engaged in a task, it probably shows he/she is nervous.

4. When a person stands erect, compared to slouching, it likely shows they are self-confident.

5. A raised eyebrow can show fear, surprise or disbelief.

6. The distance you stand away from someone while speaking to them can show how you feel about them.

7. You can judge how dominant a person is by his/her looks.

8. Books on the subject of body language can usually help you to size up others with great accuracy.

9. A person's speech rhythms can tell if they are sincere.

10. When someone pats or touches you it is sign of their submissiveness.

EXPLANATION

The spacing (item 6) that two people maintain when conversing is revealing. Normal conversation takes place over a distance of 2 or 3 feet. If, for example, you are speaking to Jane and you move in closer, she may feel uncomfortable. On the other hand, if you increase your distance, say to 4 or 5 feet this may suggest that you are distancing yourself from her.

As far as touching goes (item 10), if you're not intimate with someone the only contact that is permitted in our culture is the handshake. Anything more than that is seen as a sexual innuendo or a desire to impose status differences.

A steady eye gaze (item 1) isn't necessarily a sign of honesty. Con men usually have very steady eye fixity. In tackling a task, a confident, straightforward, person with an erect posture (item 4) and head held high, offers a firm, non-moist handshake (item 2). He/she moves about with a certain steadiness while one who is insecure is characterized by quick, rapid movements (item 3).

Status is often shown when a person pats a low status person on the back or shoulder. A subordinate would never do this to a high status person (item 10).

To Mazur, who has thoroughly studied them, books which promise to enlighten you about body language are limited in usefulness (item 8).

Lie detection experts have shown that a person's speech pace can show insecurity. A shift from a normal pace to a fast or slow pace can indicate one who is unsure about what they say. This can also include hesitations, stammering, and repetitious speech (item 9).

Our eye line can disclose our inner feelings. A lowered brow often means disapproval, anger or annoyance, while a raised brow shows fear, surprise, disbelief (item 5).

Sociologist Mazur believes it would be inaccurate to judge dominance by physical appearance (Item 7). This would include factors like a square jaw, neat attire, high forehead, good looks, etc. The most important traits are, after all, those which are invisible.

Mazur advises that body language isn't always accurate and the reliability of some of the above conclusions may vary.

SCORE

Take one point for each correct answer. Use this key:

1. False, 2. True, 3. True, 4. True, 5. True, 6. True, 7. False, 8. False, 9. True, 10. True.

8-10 points. You have above good sensitivity to non-verbal cues.

4-7 points. You have average understanding of body language cues.

3 or fewer points. You are missing important body cues that may reveal the attitudes of others.

ARE YOU ASSERTIVE ENOUGH?

With so much emphasis put on being assertive these days, it would seem that one should take a course in assertiveness training if only to be protected against all those who have already mastered it. In some social circles it is almost chic to be assertive. Although it may be overdone at times, there is still a genuine need for assertiveness in those who are repeatedly the victims of their own passivity. Their problems range from dealing effectively with the cocktail-party loudmouth to resisting the professional con artist who profits from those who can't defend themselves against his super-salesmanship.

How about you? Would you stand up and confront someone when your rights are being violated? Or are you the type to rationalize your submissiveness and call it humility?

The following quiz helps measure your degree of assertiveness.

Rate the items using this 3-point scale: 1. I wouldn't; 2. I might; 3. I definitely would. Respond to each as you would typically act in the given situations.

1. Complain when someone pushes in front of me in a line.
2. Turn down a friend's request to borrow money (say over $50).
3. Remind a good friend who seems to have forgotten that he owes me money.
4. Openly support the one I agree with when two friends argue.
5. Tell friends who visit when I want to study to return at a more convenient time.
6. When with friends, complain when food at a fancy restaurant is not satisfactory.
7. Complain to a store clerk who waits on someone who came in after me.
8. Tell someone at a meeting that their smoking annoys me.
9. Complain to my neighbor whose stereo is interfering with my sleep.
10. Complain to the parent of a child who keeps kicking the back of my seat at a movie.

SCORE

Add the numbers that correspond with the answers you gave for each item. Use this guide to find what your score means.

10-16 points. You tend to be passive when it comes to asserting your rights. You may recognize this but be unable to change your reactions. You would benefit from some assertiveness training.

17-23 points. You're average when it comes to protecting yourself or getting something from others. You have a good balance between holding back and speaking out when things frustrate you.

24-30 points. You're highly assertive. You react readily to others in terms of protecting yourself and actively claim what is coming to you. You must be careful not to go overboard when fighting for your rights. Be aware of when assertion begins to take the form of unfriendly aggression.

EXPLANATION

No one has zero assertiveness. Rather, all of us possess differing degrees of the trait. For those who are too insecure to speak out, there is assertiveness training. AT was first introduced in 1961 by a New York psychologist and author, Andrew Salter. Since then, it has gained popularity throughout the world.

The goals of AT are to increase awareness of one's personal rights and to be active in defending those rights. It teaches the difference between assertiveness and aggressiveness, the latter of which involves hostile action toward others. It has been found that low scorers on assertiveness go along with poorer emotional adjustment and insecurity.

Unfortunately, most "pop" books on AT equate being assertive with being aggressive and that's regrettable because the term can also imply expressing positive feelings like warmth, sympathy or kindness. So, a better word would be expressiveness, for it conveys positive feelings as well as those that are confrontational. Some positive assertive actions would be holding a door for someone, greeting a person or offering your seat on a bus.

IMPORTANT. If you scored low on this test, there is a strong possibility that you might be depressed. But the good news is, you can help yourself. Dr. Peter Lewisohn, in his research using AT at Indiana University, developed extensive exercises and tapes to train depressives to act more assertively and thereby, overcome their depressed states. Lewisohn's book is called *Control Your Depression*. You might want to try more assertive tactics to see if it can work for you.

MARTIN
GIUFFRE

CHAPTER 7
YOUR THINKING BRAIN

ARE YOU USING YOUR WHOLE BRAIN?

Neurosurgeon, Roger Sperry won the Nobel Prize for his proof of the split-brain theory. Because of his work it is now accepted that each half of the human brain has its own powers. The right side is the center for creative and imaginative functions, while the left side controls logic and planning. As we mature we tend to rely upon one side more than the other and develop a "brain bias."

You're using your left brain when you read this, speak to someone or add up a dinner tab, and your right brain when you listen to music, sketch a picture or imagine what you'd do if you won the lottery.

The book *Whole Brain Thinking* by Jacqueline Wonder and Patricia Donovan makes fairly definite claims about those who might feel dismayed about being "stuck" with either left or right dominance. Although, there is no difference in IQ in either right- or left-dominant persons, the authors cite many studies that show that the lazier hemisphere of the brain can be coaxed and stimulated for more versatile intellectual performance. This can be carried out through a series of brain exercises, which we'll give later.

To learn which side of your brain is dominant, take the following quiz, adapted from the book. Answer each item in terms of whether it is most like you or not. The quiz is followed by some of the authors' tips on how to develop a more balanced brain.

1. In solving a problem: a) I write out possible solutions, arrange them in order of priority, then pick out the best one; or b) I take a walk, mull things over, and then discuss it with someone.

2. a) I occasionally have hunches but don't place much faith in them; or b) I frequently have strong hunches and follow them.

3. I usually have a place for everything, a system for doing things and an ability to organize information and materials. True or false?

4. I can easily find words in a dictionary, names in a phone book, etc. True or false?

5. I learn athletics and dancing better by: a) learning the sequence and repeating the steps mentally; or b) imitating and getting the feel of the game or music.

6. I express myself well verbally. True or false?

7. When I want to remember directions, a name or news item, I: a) write notes; or b) visualize the information.

8. When I take notes, I print: a) rarely; or b) frequently.

9. I take lots of notes at a meeting or lecture. True or false?

10. When I sit in a relaxed position my hands are clasped comfortably in my lap. The thumb on top is: a) my left; or b) my right.

SCORE

To tally your score, add the "a" and "true" answers separately from the "b" and "false" answers. All "a" and "true" answers indicate left-brain dominance; all "b" and "false" answers indicate right-brain dominance.

Consider a score of 7 or more in one category to indicate dominance for that side of the brain. Should you have a close split between left and right dominance, like a 5 and 5, or a 6 and 4 score, you most likely use both sides of the brain equally.

EXPLANATIONS

You may ask how does knowing my brain dominance help me? Wonder and Donovan stress that our goal should be to lateralize the brain, i.e., to balance its use as much as possible, and thereby achieve more of our intellectual potential.

At firms like ARCO, Dow Corning and Martin Marietta, they train executives how to combine detail and logic (left-lobe functions) with a sense of overview and inventiveness (right-lobe tasks). Here are a few exercises they suggest.

To develop the right side of the brain:

Use flash forwards: Here you project yourself into future situations. For example, if you're going away, imagine yourself in the new setting. See the people around you, the surroundings, what you might be doing, etc. Flash forwards are indispensable to goal setting and inventive thinking.

Use flashbacks: Relive an event. Push yourself to recall conversations, facial expressions, colors and shapes of objects.

If you have a dream talk about it. If you have a hunch, follow it. Stretch your imagination by envisioning what you'll be doing two years from now.

To develop the left side of the brain:

Speak up: Take the chance to speak out when in front of a group.

Set goals: If you meet eight people, decide to remember the names of four of them. When you play tennis, aim to hit the ball five times in a row.

Develop time sense: Without looking at a clock estimate when five minutes have passed. Stretch it to 15 minutes, then one hour, etc. Complete a task in a definite period of time, e.g., five minutes, half an hour, etc.

Wonder and Donovan give an interesting example of right- and left-brain dominance. On Monday night football, Howard Cosell (analytic and rational) was seen as left dominant, while co-host Don Meredith, who hums tunes, tells fanciful tales, was right dominant. Between the two extremes and more lateralized, is Frank Gifford who was more evenly balanced between left and right hemispheres.

NOTE: What happens to brain dominance when one drinks? Alcohol seems to affect the right-brain before it affects the left-brain. This means that we first lose our powers of creativity and imagination when we down a martini, then later, if we continue to imbibe, our logic and speech are adversely affected.

WHAT'S YOUR DREAM I.Q.?

Dreams have intrigued mankind since Adam and Eve, and theories to explain them have been numerous. For example, it was once widely believed that they permit us to leave our bodies, wander adventurously over the earth then return safely before we awake. Dream states have taken on mystical, magical, religious and, more recently, psychiatric significance.

When Freud analyzed patients' dreams as a technique to help them overcome their problems, many experts anticipated that the dream would be the "royal road to the unconscious." But it hasn't proven to be this at all. Dreams are much more complex than even the father of psychoanalysis himself ever dreamed of.

Furthermore, if anything could frustrate psychologists, it would be that for the enormous amount of time we spend at it, we have precious few insights into our human condition based on dream research. (On average we spend about one-third of our lives sleeping and some 20 percent of that, about six years, in the dream state.) What little we know comes from work like that done by Dr. Calvin Hall of Case Western Reserve University in Cleveland, Ohio. In what was the most comprehensive study of dreams ever attempted, he analyzed some 10,000 dreams. Thousands of people were interviewed throughout the United States in Hall's survey, which asked the question: "What do essentially normal people dream of?"

Here's a chance to compare your notions about dreams with the findings of the study. Answer each item below true or false, and then check the answers.

1. Very few dreams are in color.
2. We tend to have more pleasant than unpleasant dreams.
3. Men dream more about women than they do about men.
4. We dream mostly about people who are known to us.
5. A dream event takes as long to unfold as it would if it happened in real life.
6. Our immediate surroundings can influence our dreams.
7. We can tell if a person is dreaming.
8. We can communicate with others through dreams.
9. How many dreams does the average person have each night. a) one; b) six; c) 20.
10. Dreams can help us to solve our problems.

EXPLANATIONS

1. False. About one in every three dreams reported in Hall's study was in color. Color is present more in the dreams of those who are involved with color in their daily living, e.g., fashion designers, artists, architects, etc. Color in a dream usually means that the dreamer feels strong emotion about the dream subject.

2. False. On average our unpleasant dreams outnumber those that are pleasant. In addition, as we grow older our dreams become more unpleasant. This may mean that as we age our fears about life increase, hence we have more unpleasant dreams.

3. False. Men dream more about men than about women. On the other hand, women dream equally about both sexes.

4. True. We include ourselves in almost every dream and about 85 percent of the time are joined by at least two others. According to Hall, "People who enter our dreams are generally those with whom we are emotionally involved. If you want to know who is dreaming of you, consult your own dreams."

5. False. Through a mechanism called condensation, dreams are time-distorted. What may seem a week or a year in a dream, may actually take only a few seconds.

6. True. The environment which surrounds us can easily be incorporated into our dream scenes. A man dreamed he was being tortured by his feet being held to a fire. When he suddenly awoke, he discovered his feet were resting on a hot radiator next to the bed. Or the woman who dreamed she was being beheaded. When she awoke her bed board had fallen on top of her.

7. True. Sleep researchers now rely upon a dreamer's rapid eye movement (REM) to indicate that a dream is occurring. They use special optical devices for this, but movements are usually visible through the eyelids of a sleeping person.

8. True. According to Dr. Montague Ullman there is evidence that mental telepathy can occur through dreams. In a two-year study at Maimonides Medical Center in Brooklyn, N.Y. , the noted researcher gathered evidence that a dreamer can intercept and comprehend the thoughts of others nearby.

9. B) six dreams per night.

10. True. Experiments on creativity show that "sleeping on a problem" also known as ("incubating") sometimes brings about its solution. Many creative persons reported this (writers Johann Goethe, Oliver Wendell Holmes, and mathematician H. Poincare). Through a dream, Elias Howe gained the final insight that enabled him to invent the sewing machine.

SCORE

8-10 correct. High dream IQ.

4-7 correct. Average dream IQ.

0-3 correct. Low dream IQ.

DO "WINTER BLAHS" DECK YOU?

For some otherwise hardy souls, when the summer sun fades into the gray of winter, it brings with it dramatic personality changes. Photobiologists, those who study how light affects plants and animals alike, have now identified such changes as a malady they call seasonal affective disorder (SAD). It occurs when one is deprived of sufficient daylight and it begins with the advent of winter. It brings with it three main reactions: reduced drive and motivation; mood swings; and, physiological changes. Scientists are encouraged about the connection between sunlight and health. It may even affect our immune system, making us more or less susceptible to certain diseases.

Intensive work on SAD is conducted by Harvard University Medical School, the University of Oregon, The National Institute of Mental Health in Washington, D.C. and at other centers around the United States.

Our quiz presents some of the symptoms of SAD. If your moods tend to change as winter approaches, you may be one of its unwary victims. To find out, answer Yes or No to the items, then read on.

As the days shorten from summer into winter, do you:
1. Seem to be more melancholy.
2. Tend to be more short-tempered and irritated about the actions of others.
3. Find that you grow sleepy earlier in the evening.
4. Tend to lose the enthusiasm for work which you once had.
5. Don't seem to crave seeing others as much as before.
6. Find that you desire to eat more.
7. Notice a decreased desire for affection, sex, love.
8. Usually eat more sweets.
9. Seem to need more sleep.
10. Have less energy and enthusiasm.

EXPLANATION

We've known for a long time that different wavelengths of light alter behavior. For example, pupils become erratic, restless and belligerent when red-toned fluorescent lamps are used in class. When replaced by blue-toned lamps, however, they have a pacifying affect on the children. In the animal kingdom, a bird's hormonal system in highly light sensitive and researchers have induced them to mate in the middle of winter by prolonging the lighting in their cages. Farmers have fooled the hormonal system of chickens by lengthening the day with artificial light to stimulate their egg laying.

Just how does the body interpret light which hits its surface. Dr. Alfred Lewy, director of the Sleep and Mood Disorder Lab at the University of Oregon and his colleagues, discovered melatonin, a substance secreted by the brain's pineal gland. Apparently light energy through our eyes is picked up by neural pathways and reaches this tiny light sensitive pea size gland. The pineal then produces more melatonin which lowers our mood and slows us down.

By reversing the procedure, i.e., giving light therapy (phototherapy) to those who don't receive enough sunlight, it is possible to elevate the mood levels of SAD victims.

Dr. Normal Rosenthal and colleagues at the Clinical Psychobiology Branch of N.I.M.H have treated more than 170 cases of SAD in this manner with about an 80% improvement rate. His techniques have been replicated in other parts of the world.

SCORE

The more items you answered yes, the more you're likely to experience SAD symptoms. Lest you believe that light from a floor lamp will do the trick for you, the answer is no. It doesn't contain the full spectrum of wavelengths found in natural daylight.

Lewy believes that our body rhythms are stimulated by daylight. If animals are left in the light, just 15 minutes per day, it can stabilize their body rhythms. This implies that we should all receive some natural light daily if only for a few minutes through an open window.

Keep in mind, we all have mood swings which may be due to factors other than too little daylight. Consider that SAD may be a possibility which explains your behavior only after you've ruled out all other causes.

Note: If you have trouble waking up in the morning, try leaving the shades open. The natural sunlight will help suppress your body's production of melatonin and you will be able to wake up refreshed.

HOW GOOD IS YOUR IMAGINATION?

It was Aristotle who once said that the soul (mind) never thinks without a mental picture. Increasing research tends to support this. Human thinking does indeed, involve much mental imagery.

Interviews with creative persons show that imagination almost always precedes a work of art, invention or discovery. Christopher Columbus had to imagine a world as round before he set sail on his epic voyage of discovery. Albert Einstein, who once revealed that he thought in terms of mental images and not words, had to imagine a universe where everything is relative before he theorized about the relativity of matter. It is said that he imagined riding a beam of light through the universe.

But we vary in our powers of imagination. As a matter of fact, some persons would have difficulty getting a mental picture of even so simple an object as an apple tree.

Ahead is a quiz which gauges the strength of your imagination. It is similar to those currently used to test imaginative ability.

Rate each item on a scale as follows: 1. Rarely or never; 2. Sometimes; 3. Often.

1. When I have extra time on my hands it makes me uptight and edgy.
2. I often become so absorbed in a book or movie that I lose track of time.

3. I dream more often than my friends do.

4. When it comes to books and movies, I prefer fiction to non-fiction.

5. When I retell a story I tend to embellish it with more drama for the sake of making it more interesting.

6. I can vividly imagine some extreme life situation like going to the North Pole or becoming a movie star.

7. I enjoy abstract sculpture.

8. When I awaken from a vivid dream it takes a few seconds to get back to reality.

9. I enjoy stories which involve the supernatural or sci-fi.

10. If I ever have to tell a white lie I blunder hopelessly and give myself away.

11. If I gaze at clouds or patterned wallpaper, I see images there.

12. I get a good idea for a book or film quite often.

13. I was a first-born or an only child in my family.

14. Ghost stories give me a creepy feeling.

EXPLANATION

During the past 5 decades, science has learned that imagination plays an important role not only in our thinking processes but also in our mental health. There is evidence that those who cannot imagine something or who are discouraged from using their imagination tend to develop into rigid and neurotic personalities On the other hand, too much of this activity can also be damaging. An over active imagination can lead to loss of contact with reality and to irresponsibility.

Imagining an event is often the equivalent of experiencing it in actuality. A mother, for example, waiting for a child who is very late in returning home, may suffer headaches and stress because she imagines her child in a terrible accident or an abduction. Her physical distress may be almost equal to that which she'd endure if the child were actually to fall victim to such perils.

In the field of sports psychology, imagination is used to improve an athlete's performance by having him, for example, visualize himself hitting a ball or free throwing a basketball.

In the field of mental health, some therapists use mental imagery to encourage their clients to imagine future situations of challenge in order to increase their resilience to face the upcoming event, for example, asking the boss for a raise, going out on a first date, attending a job interview or taking a plane flight.

Imaginative powers can be increased through training and the best results are with children. Professors Jerome and Dorothy Singer of Yale University have used specialized game and play exercises for this purpose. If you are a parent or work with kids, try to be on the alert for chances to "stretch" a child's imagination by simply asking him/her to imagine a future event.

SCORE

Those with high imagination tend to answer "Often" to the items. Tally your score, then consider that:

8-19 points. You are low on imagination and perhaps too concrete in your thinking. Your imagination needs stretching.

20-34 points. You are in the average range and have an adequate amount of imagination to cope with day-to-day living.

35-45 points. You have an active imagination. It's a powerful force but be careful lest you become too fanciful in your life decisions.

Note: Those who have good imaginations tend to do poorly on boring, repetitive jobs.

HOW PSYCHIC ARE YOU?

Before you read further, pick a number from this series: 1, 2, 3, 4. Later we'll explain the purpose of this.

If you ask any large number of people whether they've experienced extrasensory perception, chances are that up to half of them will say they have. You've heard the accounts—married couples who swear that they can read each other's minds, individuals who win prizes on a hunch, and those who have strong thoughts of a friend, then later get a letter or a call from that person.

Many scientists don't believe in ESP and maintain that these events can be explained by chance, natural laws and trickery. But equally as many admit that ESP may exist even though there's disputable hard evidence against it. The foremost researcher on psychic events was professor J.B. Rhine of Duke University. He found a number of traits connected with ESP powers.

The battle has been raging for about a century. Out of all this, experts have distilled a number of personality traits that are common to subjects who do well on tests of ESP and our quiz contains these traits.

If you've ever questioned whether you have ESP powers, the checklist below might provide some of the answer. Check each item which is true of you, then read on.

1. In general, you are social-oriented person who likes people and has many friends.
2. You are free of depression most of the time.
3. You have few neurotic tendencies.
4. You are in a pleasant rather than unpleasant mood most of the time.
5. You have above average ability to withstand frustration compared to your friends.
6. You are more optimistic than cynical or pessimistic.
7. You believe that there is such a thing as ESP.
8. You are a relaxed, easy-going person rather than one who is tense or high strung.
9. You are a trusting person as compared with one who is guarded and suspicious of others.
10. Sometimes your dreams have come true.

SCORE AND EXPLANATION

The frame of mind one is in when engaging in extrasensory perception is similar in nature to other altered states of consciousness such as dreaming, hypnosis, and meditation.

If you easily experience any of these states of mind, then you are also likely to be a better than average candidate for ESP as well.

A very important factor in whether or not you'll have an ESP experience is your attitude toward this phenomenon. If you strongly believe it is possible (item 7) then it will greatly influence your perception of an event. There is a powerful desire by many people to believe that the impossible is possible. Philosopher William James called this the will to believe. When someone "reads" our thoughts we may be so impressed with the correct answers he or she gives that we tend to ignore the incorrect ones.

If you'll allow an oversimplification as far as the quiz goes, the more you answered true to the items, the more likely you are to have ESP powers. Most persons should get at least 5 correct. If many of the traits describe you, then some investigators may like to hear from you. Contact The Stanford (Univ.) Research Institute, Menlo Park, Calif.; Duke University, N.C.; The American Society of Psychic Research, N.Y.; or your local college or university.

NOTE: Now about that number you picked, we'll guess it was 3. Psychological experiments show that about 70 percent of the time people pick the place position to the right of center in a series (and in our series that would be 3). If we guessed right, would you say that we had ESP powers? You might if you didn't know about series position preferences. But it wasn't any such thing.

IT'S ONLY HUMAN, OR IS IT?

How well do you know the truth about human make-up and behavior? Do you rely on many "common sense" assumptions that have been proved wrong?

Test yourself by answering the items ahead true or False.

1. Slow learners remember more than fast learners.
2. A shifty-eyed person is likely to be a liar.
3. A high forehead is a sign of a high IQ.
4. When a stranger is injured a bystander is more likely to render aid if he/she is alone than if with a group.
5. A person may inherit a talent such as ability to paint or play the violin from his parents.
6. Older people who are retired tend to be happier than oldies who still work.
7. Dull children sometimes become bright adults.
8. The blind have a sixth sense that helps them avoid obstacles.
9. Primitive people see and hear better than those in more advanced civilizations.
10. The last born in a family tends to have a higher IQ than the firstborn.
11. Older persons generally feel lonelier than those who are younger.
12. The more intelligent you are the more creative you tend to be.

ANSWERS

1. False. Slow learners usually have lower IQs than fast learners and therefore have less memory capacity. In addition, they often take longer to learn because they have difficulty comprehending what they are learning- and people remember best the things they understand.

2. False. There is no correlation between eye-gaze fixity and honesty. One study found that compared with normal persons, psychopath liars actually maintained steadier eye contact when speaking with others. A shifty-eyed person is more likely to be shy and introverted than dishonest.

3. False. Many people believe this because they think a high forehead indicates a large brain. But craniotomy studies do not show any correlations between forehead size and intelligence. The size of a normally developed brain is also not related to intelligence, a person with a 3-pound brain may be brighter than one with a brain of 5 pounds.

4. True. Bystanders feel indecisive about assuming individual responsibility when under group influence, possibly out of fear of criticism. However, they are more willing to act when the victim is solely dependent on them in a one-to-one relationship.

5. False. A person inherits nothing from his parents or ancestors beyond his biological makeup and perhaps two or three instincts. All of our human capabilities develop principally through learning from others.

6. False. Happiness questionnaires given to retirees show no differences between them and those who are still employed.

7. False. Although a dull child's IQ may increase several points if placed in a stimulating setting, he will rarely, if ever, reach a superior level in adulthood. Occasionally, a child with an undetected brain disorder will test for years at the dull normal level (IQ between 70 and 90). When the condition is corrected, intelligence may shoot up to high average or superior levels. But this is very rare. By the way, some kids who make low grades in their earlier years may suddenly improve later. But the change is usually due to situational or emotional factors and not to an increase in intelligence.

8. False. Although the blind have no special senses, those that they retain become more highly developed (trained) then those of sighted persons. A classic study at Cornell University found that the blind use their sense of hearing as bats do. To some extent, they develop the ability to avoid bumping into obstacles through a sonar-like sensitivity to sound-wave frequencies to which their ears have become attuned.

9. False. How efficiently we use our senses depends upon how we are trained to use them. A native guide distinguishes subtleties in the jungle because his senses have been trained to look for them. If given a stethoscope, however, he would miss (as most of us probably would) the subtleties in a heartbeat, which the ear of a physician has been trained to detect.

10. False. Studies on birth order and intelligence have been numerous and conflicting. But an outstanding analysis by Dr. Zack Rubin of nearly 400,000 19 year-old males in Holland, disclosed that IQ decreases from first to last born. No one really knows why. Some experts theorize that a firstborn benefits from better prenatal development, or that he is intellectually

more stimulated because he has his parents to himself for longer than his later-born siblings do.

11. False. Surveys done at New York University and the University of California (LA) show that even though more old people than young live alone, the elderly are more satisfied with their friendships, feel more independent and have a higher sense of self-esteem. Young persons, on the other hand, are often pressured to "find a special someone" and feel unhappy if they cannot. The surveys show that young singles and the recently divorced were the loneliest.

12. False. Creative ability, like imagination, is neither related to nor dependent upon intelligence. One researcher, for example, found no relationship between the creativity of scientists and their intelligence scores.

SCORE

Take one point for each correct answer.

A score of 0-4 is low. You must challenge your untested assumptions about human nature. We recommend more reading on the subject.

A score of: 5-9 is average. You do make faulty judgments about others from time to time, which might cause you difficulty.

A score of 10-12 is high. Compared to others, you have a good understanding of human nature.

ARE YOU A SAVVY SHOPPER?

The Romans had a term for it: *Caveat Emptor* - let the buyer beware. And, in these days of rising inflation, that nugget of advice is timelier than ever. A wise shopper is one who can "psych" out those wily merchants who try to squeeze out maximum profit for their wares and services.

This quiz tests your smarts in the marketplace. It also gives pointers on how to save some of your hard-earned cash.

Answer True or False to the items then read on for explanations.

1. It is wiser to shop for groceries before rather than after eating.

2. Private brands are usually a better deal than nationally advertised ones.

3. It's not a good idea to seek other medical opinions since it will hurt your relationship with your doctor.

4. It is cheaper to buy clothes for durability rather than for style.

5. Stores which offer special sales are usually the best places to shop for mostly all items.

6. It costs less to cash a large out-of -town check than to deposit it in your checking or savings account.

7. Coin-op dry cleaning is a better buy than the professional variety.

8. You'll come out ahead if you ask your physician to prescribe generic rather than brand name drugs.

9. Despite the jokes about it, when shopping for a car it's helpful to slam the doors as a simple test of solidity.

10. Although some shoppers are impulse buyers, stores depend on them for significant profits.

11. To a discerning shopper, the way "best buy" items are displayed has little effect on them.

12. It's better to plan just one weekly visit to the supermarket than to make a few trips there.

EXPLANATION

1. False. Motivation experts find that people who shop for groceries before eating tend to make more impulse buys and bring home more than they need.

2. True. Private brands of equal quantity and quality compared to highly advertised national brands usually cost less.

3. False. It pays to get other diagnostic viewpoints even if you run the remote risk of ruffling your doctor. Government studies show that a large number of operations are incorrect and unnecessary.

4. False. Clothes are fashion-oriented and the psychology of large numbers of consumers is to discard many items or use them less frequently after the first season of wear.

5. False. Specials are often loss leaders. It's well known that stores make up for these losses by hiking prices on other things.

6. False. There is usually a collection fee for cashing a check.

7. True. Coin-ops are set up for bulk cleaning (by the pound) rather than by the garment, therefore, they cost considerably less.

8. Despite heavy and persuasive advertising of brand name drugs, generics are invariably cheaper.

9. False. Car builders are aware that the public believes this and they try to build a solid sound into their door slams.

10. True. Almost all bad buys are made in a hurry. Impulse buying accounts for a hefty 10-15% of profits. Items more apt to be purchased on impulse are placed in the front of the store because one is more likely to buy impulsively when the shopping cart is empty.

11. False. Merchandisers spend plenty to study exactly how items should be displayed. It is well known that "eye level is buy level." Also toys and food, which appeal to kids, are often put on low shelves so they can reach them.

12. False. A single trip, of say more than 3/4 hours tends to create "supermarket hypnosis." Camera research finds that eye blinking slows up measurably with time and can lead to slower reflexes and impaired judgment. Faced with so many shelves of products, the brain numbs and causes us to overbuy. In this state of mind, experts say "every minute over 30 is worth fifty cents from a shopper."

SCORE

For your consumer IQ, tote up your score.

10-12 points. You are an alert shopper who knows what to look for and how to save dollars.

5-9 points. You are squarely in the consumer majority.

0-4 points. You lack basic consumer know-how. Don't despair, unlike your true IQ, your score can be raised. Just keep reading those consumer advice columns when they come your way or better still, subscribe to a consumer magazine and also search the internet for information on various products.

WHAT IS YOUR FAMILY IQ?

Cartoons have that unique quality of telescoping large meanings into small pictures. There's the one that shows an Arab teen and his father inside their oasis tent. The boy asks beseechingly: "Dad, can I please have the camel tonight?"

Should you conclude that home life is the same the world over after seeing this, you'd only be slightly right. For around the globe, families show some unusual differences that would surprise you.

Anthropologist George P. Murdock, author of *Social Structure*, an outstanding sociological treatise, researched some 250 cultures and came up with noteworthy findings. Test yourself on how much you know about families from other cultures. Answer each item either true or false.

1. The husband assumes the authority role in the family in most societies throughout the world.

2. All cultures have a system that allows the breakup of a marriage.

3. Primitive societies have fewer marital splits than those in industrialized countries.

4. Premarital sex is frowned upon throughout the world.

5. Most cultures are monogamous.

6. The weaker the family unit, the more likely its members will join outside radical and deviant groups.

7. Some societies allow adultery.

8. In most cultures men initiate sexual actions toward women more often than vice versa.

9. Virtually all societies disapprove of divorce.

10. Some cultures permit incest.

11. The family and the institution of marriage exist in every known human society.

12. Divorces are most likely after the 7th year of marriage.

EXPLANATION AND ANSWERS

1. True. The father is universally seen as the dominant figure, even in those lands where women's liberation has taken a strong hold. He is expected to provide material support and authority and his wife, to provide affection and moral support.

2. True. All cultures allow couples to split if the going becomes too difficult. Divorce fluctuates with the economy, up in prosperity, down in depression.

3. False. The rate of marital misses is actually greater among pre-industrial ("primitive") societies than for, example, in the United States and other Western nations.

4. False. Of all cultures Murdock studied, 70 percent (158) allowed premarital sex. In his book, *New Rules,* pollster Daniel Yankelovich compiled data from numerous surveys and found that some 63% of parents of college youths condoned premarital sex, providing the partners were in love.

5. True. A few allow more than one wife to a husband (polygamy) but none permit more than one husband to a wife. Having more than one wife is usually found in the upper classes and is considered a badge of distinction.

6. True. As family bonds weaken, it's likely that its members will gravitate to outside groups whose values are more liberal or radical then those of the family.

7. False. Only five societies in the sample of 258 freely condone adultery.

8. False. Among modern nations it has been traditionally usual for men to take the initiative in sex. But if you include flirting and other such invitational gestures, men and women are equal with regard to assertiveness in sexual activity in the majority of societies studied.

9. True. Most societies show social disapproval of divorce.

10. False. There are strong taboos against incest worldwide.

11. True. There isn't a single society that does not recognize the family and marriage as the basic foundation of its culture.

12. False. At least in the U.S., the timing of a marital rupture reaches a peak around the third year. After the first few months of marriage, the risk quickly rises to reach a maximum during the third year.

SCORE

Take a point for each correct answer.

As a rule, married people do better on tests about family matters than do single people. If you scored: 10 points or higher. You have an excellent grasp of family-life norms as they exist in foreign lands.

5-9 points. You have an average knowledge of the subject.

0-4 points. You're in the dark when it comes to knowing about family life and traditions, globally that is. If you're seriously contemplating marriage to someone of a different nationality, it might be wise to do some reading on the subject before tying the knot,

"Which of you gentlemen is the woodpecker?"

CHAPTER 8

YOUR EMOTIONAL WELLNESS

ARE YOU SAAVY ABOUT HEALTH ISSUES? PART 1

True or False:

1. Drinking 8 glasses or more of water daily is healthy and will prevent kidney stones.
2. Some people can be carriers of diseases without ever appearing sick.
3. Your heart stops for an instant whenever you sneeze.
4. Taking vitamin C will help you avoid getting a cold.
5. Wearing a copper bracelet can cure arthritis.
6. We use only 10 percent of our brains.
7. Cold, wet weather will not cause colds and flu.
8. Food eaten late at night is more fattening.
9. Reading in dim light ruins your eyesight.
10. If you eat too many carrots, your skin will turn yellow.

ANSWERS

1. False. Dr. Alex Finkbeiner, (University of Arkansas Medical Society) concludes there is no basis for this belief. He advises people to simply let their thirst guide their fluid intake. But water can reduce kidney stone formation so drink enough to keep your urine looking like water. Avoid letting it turn dark.

2. True. Some germs cause asymptomatic infection, i.e., a person can have the "germ" in their body, but don't have disease symptoms. Dr. Anupama Menon of UAMS. explains, "the particular virus or bacteria can then be transmitted by a cough or sneeze, to others . . . but carriers usually don't have the virus or bacteria in their system for a prolonged period of time, though."

3. False. Dr Chris Danner of UAMS says a sneeze, causes the chest pressure to decrease venous blood flow back to the heart. The heart compensates for this by a slight change in its beating rate, but its electrical activity should not stop during a sneeze.

4. False. Vitamin C (ascorbic acid) is good for preventing scurvy, but it won't prevent colds according to Dr. Charles Born of the UAMS. The vitamin may reduce the severity of symptoms, but evidence is unclear. Born says, "Taking it over long periods of time in large amounts may actually be harmful, it may cause severe diarrhea, a particular danger for the elderly and children."

5. False. Arthritis is a loss of the joint surface cartilage. Vendors propose that the copper is absorbed through the skin and helps cartilage regeneration. "But," says Dr. Randy Bindra of the Center for Hand and Upper Extremity Surgery at UAMS, "it is not easily absorbed in this way. we require very small amounts of it." Further, copper deficiency is extremely rare and most regular diets provide enough of it

6. False. This is a bogus notion. Dr. Rachel Vreeman (Indiana University School of Medicine) states that brain imaging studies show that no area of the brain is completely inactive. Detailed probing of the brain has failed to identify the "non-functioning" 90 percent.

7. False. Colds are caused by viruses, with enough variations to give you a choice of 200 versions of a cold. You can get a virus through inhaling infected air droplets sneezed or coughed by others or by contacting something they touched and then transferring germs to your mouth or nose.

8. False. Studies at the Dunn Nutrition Centre in Cambridge, Mass. suggest the belief that you will store more fat because it is not burned off with any activity at night is a myth—it's the total amount eaten in a 24-hour period that's important, But it is true that people who skip meals during the day, then eat loads in the evening are more likely to be overweight.

9. False. "This notion probably has its origins in eye strain," says Dr. Aaron Carroll of Indiana University Medical School. Bad lighting makes it hard to focus, makes you blink less and get dry eyes, particularly if you're squinting. Though uncomfortable it doesn't cause permanent damage. "A hundred years ago we read by candlelight and weren't going blind," says Carroll. "There's no evidence for this whatsoever."

10. True. Eating too many carrots, or other foods high in beta-carotene, can cause a condition called carotenemia, explains Dr. Jerri Hoskyn (University of Arkansas). "This can result in a yellowish skin discoloration most noticeable on the palms and soles. Unlike jaundice, though, carotenemia does not cause yellowing of the eyes. It usually is seen in young children, is not toxic and generally does not cause other health problems. The treatment is a low-carotene diet, but it may take several months for the skin to return to its normal color.

SCORE
Take a point for each correct answer:

1-3 points. Low. You need to read more articles and watch more TV health programs.

4-7 points. Average. You know as much about health as most of us, but more knowledge would help.

8-10 points. High. You'd exceed some 90% of those who would take this test. Keep learning more.

ARE YOU SAAVY ABOUT YOUR HEALTH? PART 2

TRUE OR FALSE:

1. Chocolate causes acne.
2. You can catch a venereal disease (STD) by using a public restroom.
3. Shaving hairs causes them to grow back faster, darker and coarser.
4. Breast size influences how much breast milk you can produce.
5. Breast size influences breast cancer rates or prognosis.
6. Staring at an eclipse can blind you.
7. Drinking warm milk helps to put you to sleep.
8. The risk of dying from cancer in the U.S. is increasing.
9. If you are healthy, your lifestyle as a young adult has little to do with getting cancer later in life.
10. Women get drunk faster than men.

ANSWERS

1. False. Loraine Stern, MD of UCLA says the link between chocolate intake and acne outbreaks has been broken. Other studies, however, show that stress can cause outbreaks when the oil glands make too much sebum, a waxy substance that can clog pores.

2. False. Dr. Mary J. O'Sullivan, of the University of Miami, says the idea that you could get an STD from a toilet seat "sounds believable," but is highly unlikely. Hard surfaces such as toilet seats are not conducive to STDs.

3. False. Wax, shave or cut—no matter how you remove your hair, you won't change its texture or speed of growth. "Leg hair will, however, appear coarser right as it starts to grow back. Initially it is blunt, and hasn't had time to taper off, so it might look darker," says Carroll. But as it grows and is exposed to the sun, it will look exactly like the hair you started with.

4. False. Because breast size depends more on the amount of supporting fibrous and fatty tissue than the number of milk glands, women with larger breasts do not necessarily produce more breast milk.

5. False. Breast size does not affect your risk of breast cancer. The most common type of breast cancer comes from cells lining the ducts of the milk-producing glands. Since women with larger breasts do not necessarily have more gland tissue, they do not run a higher risk, but obesity increases the risk because greater amounts of fat tissue increase the estrogen level.

6. True. Sunlight can damage the light-sensitive nerve endings in the back of the eye (retina) causing vision loss. Never view the sun directly with the naked eye or with any unfiltered device, such as binoculars or a telescope!

7. True. Milk contains the sleep-inducing substance tryptophan.

8. False. The diagnosis of cancer each year has indeed grown because the U.S. population is growing and aging. Dr. Ted Gansler, (American Cancer Society) reports the numbers by age group show that cancer risk for Americans is actually dropping.

9. False. Dr. Gansler says most cases of cancer are the consequence of many years of exposure to several risk factors. What you eat, whether you are physically active, whether you get sunburned regularly and especially, whether you smoke as a young person have a strong influence on whether you develop cancer later in life.

10. True. Women's bodies have a lower percentage of water than men's and therefore reach a higher blood alcohol concentration faster. And that's not all. Women have half the amount of gastric alcohol dehydrogenase, a compound that breaks down alcohol. Because women aren't as efficient in digesting alcohol, a greater amount of alcohol hits the bloodstream and goes straight to the brain.

SCORE
Take a point for each correct answer.

1-3 points. Low. You need to read more articles and watch more TV health programs.

4-7 points. Average. You know as much about health as most of us, but more knowledge would help.

8-10 points. High. You'd exceed some 90% of those who would take this test. Keep learning more.

NOTE: If you scored low on both parts of this test, it would be wise to learn more on health. Attend lectures, read good books and articles, and yes, even ask your doctor more questions.

ARE YOU OR IS SOMEONE YOU KNOW A SMOKING ADDICT?
The United States Surgeon General has made public, findings which further condemn tobacco as a consumer product. It cannot be too far off when it will be unlawful to smoke in public places.

As far as the psychology of smoking goes, a considerable number of smokers who can't seem to kick the habit are victims of their own denial. They labor under a "guiding fiction" which says, "Yes, I know I smoke, but if I really wanted to, I could voluntarily quit at any time."

But without some outside influence, this may not be as easy as it seems. The fact is that many smokers are hidden addicts and don't know it.

Ahead is a quiz which might shed some light on the matter. It was adapted from a booklet published by Bristol-Myers (pharmaceutical company) and written by psychiatrist Dr. Norman E. Zinberg of the Harvard Medical School.

If you or someone you know smokes, consider offering it. It just might help them to recognize a problem they've been denying up to now. Answer the items as follows: Yes, Sometimes, or No.

1. I have a cigarette with a cup of coffee or after a meal.

2. I find that I've lit and smoked a cigarette without having made a conscious decision to do so.

3. Stairs or hills seem hard to climb lately.

4. I light up a cigarette when I'm angry or upset.

5. I smoke to perk myself up.

6. I am quite anxious when I discover that I've run out of cigarettes.

7. I have a cough in the morning when I wake up.

8. I light up a cigarette while another is lit in the ashtray.

9. I smoke more than 12 cigarettes each day.

10. When you say to friends, "I only smoke occasionally", do they laugh?

11. When someone lights up, I feel a strong urge to also smoke.

12. My everyday routines are based on a break for coffee and a cigarette, for example.

EXPLANATION:

The quiz you just took should help you recognize the early signs of addictive smoking behavior. When addicted we become deeply dependent and controlled by a physical substance. Certain tissue groups within the body, through a very complex biochemical process, learn to crave the substance for their continued functioning and find it difficult to metabolize without it.

SCORE

Consider that if you responded "yes" or "sometimes" to five or more of the items above, you are probably an addicted smoker.

GETTING STARTED

When you attempt to quit, you may need special help to cope with your body's desire for nicotine. Nicotine replacement therapy can help some smokers control withdrawal symptoms as they quit. You can buy some nicotine replacement products over-the-counter. Nicotine replacement therapy methods such as chewing gum, skin patches, tablets, nasal sprays, or inhalers ease withdrawal symptoms such as cravings and mood changes. Bupropion (trade name Zyban), which does not contain nicotine, can help an addicted smoker resist the urge to smoke. Studies show that these methods can almost double the chances of breaking a smoking addiction.

Check with your doctor first to see if one is a good choice for you. He or she might recommend one of the over-the-counter forms.

Accountability lends support. Do not try conquering your smoking addiction on your own. If at all possible, join a friend or group also trying to kick the habit and monitor your progress together.

Lastly, pinpoint habits or locations that are associated with smoking and change the routine. Don't give up. Full victory may come after a relapse. Try again, bearing in mind what might have triggered the setback.

TRUE OR FALSE: A LITTLE DRINKING HELPS YOUR THINKING

Note: On any test, there's always the chance that our precede might clue you in to what the quiz measures and cause you (unwittingly or not) to slant your answers. To see if this is so, ask someone who knows you well to take the quiz with you in mind, and then compare your answers.

It would be hard for Americans to agree that "'water is the only drink for a wise man,'" as Henry David Thoreau once advised, for we consume over 2 billion gallons of wine, beer and liquor yearly. No doubt about it, brothers and sisters, we are a drink-oriented society.

As a social lubricant, alcohol has become the unprecedented elixir of elation for some 95 million of us who practice the gentle but untutored art of elbow bending. Some of us are at a point where we can't live with it or without it.

There is so much of the heady nectar surrounding us, yet surprisingly little is known about alcohol and its effects on our actions. Take the following quiz to learn some interesting facts about the world of spirits.

Answer the following items TRUE or FALSE, or choose the right answer.

1. Alcohol increases the sex drive.

2. A can of beer is less intoxicating than an ounce of liquor.

3. You can tell when a person has had too much to drink by the way he walks and talks.

4. How many alcoholics are there in the United States? (a) 5 million; (b) 10 million, or (c) 50 million.

5. What percentage of patients are in our city hospitals for alcohol-related reasons? (a) one out of 20, (b) one out of 10, or (c) one out of two.

6. Although they live unhappy lives, alcoholics tend to live slightly longer than non-alcoholics.

7. Some alcohol helps you to be more alert and to think better.

8. If you can't tolerate much liquor, the best way to avoid becoming drunk is to shun alcohol altogether.

9. Men have more drinking problems than women.

10. Alcohol tends to increase self-confidence and reduce one's fears.

ANSWERS AND EXPLANATION

Tally your score by reading the answers and explanations below to find out how much you know about alcohol and its effects.

1. False. It's an old wives' tale that alcohol improves sex. But it's a young wives' tale that complains that men are less effective sexually after they drink. Alcohol increases the desire but diminishes the performance.

2. False. A 12-ounce can of beer, a 1-ounce shot of 100 proof liquor and a 6-ounce glass of wine are equal in their effect on the body.

3. False. Many persons who are mentally impaired from alcohol do stagger or slur their words. Alcohol seems to have a delayed reaction on their speech, muscles and locomotion.

4. (b) The U.S. Public Health Service estimates there are some 10 million alcoholics in the United States. Some experts say it's as high as 20 million (1.3 million are teens between 12 and 17 years old).

5. (c) One out of two.

6. False. Alcoholics die 10 to 12 years sooner than non-alcoholics.

7. False. Even in minute amounts, alcohol is a neural depressant. It promotes relaxation by inhibiting certain nerve centers but it retards reaction time as well as brain functions.

8. False. You may not realize it, but you could be drinking too quickly. The body can clear about three-fourths of an ounce of alcohol from the blood in one hour. So, if you're of medium build and don't exceed this rate, you can still enjoy an evening of social drinking.

9. True. U.S. Public Health Service statistics disclose more male than female alcoholics. But the female rate is rising. It is also true that the number of housewives who quietly drink at home is increasing.

10. True. Alcohol gives a false sense of confidence and it increases risk taking. According to the Life Skills Education Group in Weymouth, Mass., when a group of bus drivers were given several drinks, they were willing to drive through spaces too narrow for their vehicles. Their judgment was adversely affected by alcohol and they were more willing to risk failure compared to when they were not drinking.

SCORE
If you got at least five correct, you're at the head of the class. When these items were given to a representative sample of college students, the average number of "hits" was only four.

DO YOU HAVE HURTFUL EATING HABITS?
Scientists tell us that hunger is an automatic body response that signals us when to eat. But what we eat, how often and how much is another matter. The choices, all too often, depend upon our personality, our conditioning, and how we feel at a given time.

Depression, stress, anxiety, etc. can upset our eating patterns. And we know that television commercials can influence children's appetites, i.e. kids are conditioned to crave certain foods.

It is likely that occasionally, at least, what and how you eat isn't in line with what your body needs for healthy functioning. Richard Kozlenko, M.D., who practices holistic medicine in Mill Valley, Calif., has studied the harmful effects of emotion upon our eating habits and our general nutritional well-being, He developed a health-evaluation survey that assesses how feelings interfere with healthy eating. The survey attempts to answer the question: Are you relatively free to choose the foods that are truly good for you or are your eating habits distorted by your emotions?

If you wonder whether your eating patterns are healthy, the following quiz, adapted from Kozlenko's survey, should provide an answer. Answer each item as follows:

1 point. Seldom (5 to 10 times a year)

2 points. Occasionally (2 to 3 times a month)

3 points. Frequently (daily or every other day)

1. I tend to overeat or under eat when I feel blue or bored.
2. I engage in between-meal binges, consuming large amounts of food at one sitting.
3. I have a craving for sweets.
4. I eat meals or heavy snacks after 7 p.m.
5. I eat when I am not hungry.
6. I often overeat
7. I eat rapidly when under pressure.
8. I eat junk foods.
9. I get uncontrollable hunger urges.
10. When I am agitated or worried, I eat to calm down or am unable to eat.

EXPLANATIONS

There is evidence that if left to themselves animals will leisurely eat a balanced and limited amount of food to sustain themselves. Pregnant rats, for example, will increase their intake of protein and calcium; those with vitamin B deficiencies choose foods rich in that vitamin; and animals experimentally deprived of salt will naturally increase their intake of salty foods. But it's different with humans. Strong cultural influences such as the media, social customs, strong family traditions, etc., block natural instincts that signal what and how much to eat. Our acquired tastes for candy, cola and potato chips are simply not in accord with our bodily needs.

A classic study done by Dr. Clara M. Davis showed that human beings, when left completely free, choose a balanced diet. For periods ranging from six months to four years, Davis allowed weaned 6-month-olds plenty of time to select the food and the amount they desired from a variety of foods presented on trays set before them. In this so-called "cafeteria-feeding" scheme, all foods were painstakingly measured and the health and weight of each baby was carefully checked periodically.

The results were conclusive. All babies thrived on a diet of their own choosing, which was not widely different from those recommended by nutrition experts. The babies' growth was in advance of standard growth tables and no bad effects of any kind were noted. As a matter of fact, one baby suffering from rickets chose cod-liver oil-saturated foods (rich in vitamin D) and cured himself.

The babies were responding to their "body wisdom," a term coined by famed physiologist Dr. Walter B. Cannon of Harvard University to describe the self-regulating process by which our bodies remain healthy.

SCORE

To find out what your score is and what it indicates, tally the numbers that correspond with the answers you gave for each item, and then read the following categories:

10-15 points. You have good control over your eating habits and are in tune with your body's needs for food intake.

16-20 points. You fall within the average range for healthy people with sensible eating habits.

21-30 points. You have excessive emotional interference with your eating habits. Perhaps a visit to a nutritional counselor is in order.

THE BEST WAY TO FLY IS BY TRAIN.
(ABOUT PHOBIAS-TAKE THIS QUIZ FOR FUN)

The late Jackie Gleason, known to have a flying phobia, once made this quip. Gleason wasn't alone. As many as 8 out of 10 people in the United States suffer from some type of phobia. The condition is an intense and irrational fear, the most common of which is agoraphobia, a dread of open or public places. Some two and a half million suffer from it, among whom was Sigmund Freud himself.

How much do you know about phobias, one of America's most pervasive afflictions? Take the quiz ahead, then read on.

1. Cainophobia: a) fear of sticks and poles; b) fear of dogs; c) dread of change or novelty.
2. Doraphobia: a) fear of small boats; b) fear of touching animals; c) fear of dumb girls.
3. Pantophobia: a) fear of everything; b) fear of cooking utensils; c) fear of beggars.
4. Bogyphobia: a) a dread of demons and goblins; b) fear of false ideas; c) strong aversion to private-detective movies.
5. Dinophobia: a) fear of eating out; b) fear of dinosaurs; c) fear of whirlpools.
6. Ballistophobia: a) fear of being hit by a ball; b) aversion to dancing; c) fear of missiles.
7. Sitiophobia: a) powerful reluctance to crouch; b) abnormal dread of food; c) fear of the city.
8. Cynophobia: a) fear of being poisoned; b) fear of dogs; c) dread of the color blue.

EXPLANATION

The difference between normal fears and phobias is twofold: First, a phobia is usually obsessional in nature, i.e., one is preoccupied with it. Second, the phobic person overreacts to his anxiety and often freezes up in a phobic situation. For example, a person with normal fear of water might subdue the fear enough to learn to swim, but a phobic might avoid learning to swim altogether. Just why phobias form is still a mystery. Some experts believe they are tied to specific events. For example, one who escapes a burning house might develop a phobia for fires. But thousands of persons in fires don't have phobias, so other elements in a traumatic event must cause phobias.

The most popular theory of how phobias take hold is based on social learning. A main proponent of this view is Professor Albert Bandura of Stanford University, who argues that we learn phobias through others.

Thus a 2-year-old whose mother screams when she sees a spider might herself develop a fear of spiders, because she experiences the same fear within herself as her mother does at that moment.

SCORE
Give yourself a point for each correct answer.

Answers: 1-C; 2-B; 3-A; 4-A; 5-C; 6-C; 7-B; 8-B.

You did well if you scored a 3 or better — unless, of course, you have a phobia about taking quizzes.

DO YOU UNDERSTAND LONELINESS?
We live in an age of interpersonal awareness, yet loneliness persists in our fast-paced society. Often, cultivating genuine friendships can be a frustrating experience. Has our world become so complex and changeable that loneliness must be a necessary by-product of today's lifestyle?

If you've ever had the painful sense of isolation, of being lost in crowd, you're not alone. Seeds of loneliness are present in all of us and is an inevitable part of living.

The quiz explores a number of mistaken notions about loneliness. Answer each of the items true or false, and then match your answers with those of behavior experts at the end of the quiz.

1. Loneliness generally increases as we grow older.

2. Lonely people are often well-adjusted types who just can't seem to meet others.

3. A person's loneliness is a personal matter and our society has little to do with it.

4. Those who live alone are more prone to loneliness than those who live with someone.

5. The older a child is when his parents are divorced, the less lonely he will be later in life.

6. Wealth, occupation and education are relatively unimportant when it comes to feeling lonely.

7. Loneliness is easier to bear if you feel that many other people are lonely too.

8. Singles are more likely to be lonely in old age.

9. Dislocations caused by job changes, moves or shifts in lifestyles are major causes of loneliness.

10. Loneliness is an inborn trait of temperament which many people have that can't be changed very much.

EXPLANATION

1. False. Surveys conducted at New York University and the University of California at Los Angeles show that even though more seniors than young people live alone, the elderly are more satisfied with their friendships, and have a higher sense of self-esteem. The surveys showed that young singles and the recently divorced were the loneliest.

2. False. On the contrary, many lonely persons are self-defeating. They withdraw, remain solitary, or don't take the admitted risk of reaching out to others. Shyness, fear of rejection and lack of self-esteem are contributing factors.

3. False. Philip Slater, in his social critique, *The Pursuit of Loneliness*, suggests that our competitive, self-oriented society promotes isolation. Another cause of loneliness is the "me-generation" attitude, which concentrates on self-development and not so much on giving ourselves to others.

4. False. Actually the social and personal lives of the lonely and not lonely aren't so far apart. What is important is the attitude of those who constantly complain of loneliness. A sense of dissatisfaction dominates their lives regardless of how many people they know. Friends, spouses and partners somehow fail to satisfy their needs for love and companionship.

5. True. A divorce is always an unhappy time for a child. Those younger than 6 at the time of separation ranked much higher on loneliness later in life. The older child seems better able to adjust to loss or change with less upset in later life.

6. False. One's socioeconomic situation does make a difference. The surveys showed that the loneliest people are likely to be poor, uneducated, underemployed and minority group members.

7. True. If everyone around us is unhappy and alone we can more readily accept our plight; there is some solace in group suffering. But if others appear happy and carefree, our own lonely feelings by contrast become magnified and intense.

8. False. This is a popular notion but the facts don't support it. Singles develop interests and patterns of living that compensate for lack of companionship. As a result, they are less likely to be lonely later on than one who had a family and is now widowed.

9. False. The opposite, in fact, may be true. The studies show that such dislocations can cause temporary isolation, but that people who move often out of necessity, actually become adept at making new friends easily.

10. False. There are some conflicting conclusions from various studies, but in most cases, loneliness can be overcome. When a society acknowledges the causes of loneliness in its members; when people can recognize their loneliness and guide themselves away from it, the painful experience of it can be reduced and overcome.

SCORE

8 or more correct. You have a realistic grasp of the roots of loneliness. Compared with low scorers, you're in the best position to get along with those who are lonely and to help yourself when loneliness strikes.

4-7 correct. You are solidly in the average range as far as knowing what causes loneliness. You make some errors handling this condition in yourself or others, but most of the time it won't be a major problem.

3 or less correct. You're blocked by false assumptions about loneliness. Lonely people might feel misunderstood by you. Some reading on the subject will help you deal better with this common malady of mankind.

COPING WITH LONELINESS - TEN TIPS

Loneliness isn't easy to conquer if it's caused by a person's poor self-image. When you're down on yourself, you tend to avoid others. There are certain proven techniques which can be helpful.

1. When seeking new friendships start with the known then work toward the unknown. Stay in your own back yard. Your church or synagogue is a good place to begin. Scan your local newspapers, bulletin boards of libraries and community centers for local events which seem promising and attend as many as you can. You'll feel safer when you're on home turf especially where there are a few familiar faces in the crowd.

2. Reach out to those who need and will appreciate you. Do volunteer work with children, senior citizens, and those in hospitals, etc. Contact groups like the Red Cross, American Cancer Society, the Community Aid Society, and various health care agencies. You'll find others there who are also seeking friends.

3. Dr. Alan Fromme used to teach his clients to "make a habit of people" and to keep moving. Don't wait for someone to call. Take the initiative and phone someone yourself. At the beginning of each week make a list of at least 10 things to do which will bring you into contact with people. Now grade these in order of difficulty.

You could: have friends over for a drink, coffee or dinner; be Big Sister/Brother to a needy youngster; enroll in a lecture series or a book discussion group; join your chamber of commerce; attend a church meeting; have coffee with a neighbor; chat with a grocery store clerk, in brief, do anything which will help break your pattern of isolation from others.

4. Try for the unusual. Search for interesting people and try to be different in your approach. Don't be caught in the conventional rat race. Seek out novel situations, i.e., art shows, antique fairs, church suppers, auctions, receptions, political gatherings, homecoming rallies, and so on.

If you aren't turned on by a particular event such as an antique auto show, keep in mind that your focus is on people and the event is merely a door opener to new faces.

5. Before you attend a function, practice openers. If you feel uneasy about new settings and about meeting strangers, rehearse your lines in advance. Keep a few jokes or funny stories on tap which have relevance to the group you're meeting. Store away some newsy items, then when the right moment comes in a conversation, sing them out.

6. Practice being a good listener. Don't be a conversation hog. Give the other person a chance to express him or herself. People who are popular are those who know how to show interest in others by listening carefully.

7. Let your skills and interests work for you. Take careful inventory of those activities in which you have some ability or strong interest. You'll probably be surprised at how many you'll come up with. The list might include: photography, jogging, bike riding, needlepoint, antiquing, decorating, nature study, sketching, skiing, cooking, bridge, hiking, chess, etc. Then look under "social organizations" and "clubs" in the yellow pages and select the best ones to join. (The New York City directory, for example lists over five pages of such groups.)

In general, try to develop skills, interests and hobbies which you can share with others.

8. Don't turn down any chance, no matter how trivial, to interact with someone. This means doing little things like buying someone lunch, accompanying a friend to the dentist, complimenting a person about his or her clothes.

9. Until you're out of your lonely doldrums, try to avoid those who are themselves pessimistic, lonely or gloomy. They'll influence you more than you might realize. On the contrary, do try to be with live wires—those who are animated, active, and have a positive attitude about life.

10. Finally, remember, even though they may not show it, all persons grow lonely occasionally. Even if your heart isn't in it, say to yourself; "these techniques have worked for others and some of them should work for me too."

DOES THE BLACK DOG HOUND YOU? (DEPRESSION BLUES)

Winston Churchill called his occasional melancholy the black dog. It submerged him to the depths of despair. No matter what our station in life, many of us become distressed at one time or another. The mood can range from a bout of blues to a disabling psychological illness.

In 2002, according to the National Institute of Mental Health, some 10 million Americans sought treatment for depression. It's not an uncommon state of mind. Even in the most secure of societies, where pressure is at a minimum, depression is found to be a normal reaction to setbacks in life goals. So, if you do get a case of the blues now and then, you're not alone by any means.

To estimate how much you know about depression, and perhaps pick up a tip or two on how to cope with it, answer True or False to the items, then read on for an explanation.

TRUE OR FALSE

1. Most forms of depression are easy to recognize.

2. Your diet can affect your moods.

3. Depression is psychological and can't be detected in clinical tests.

4. No one has ever died of love sickness, no matter how heart broken they were over their last romance.

5. You can inherit a depression tendency from your parents.

6. Depression is more common in men than in women.

7. A little alcohol can lift your mood.

8. Exercise, as healthful as it is, won't affect depression much.

9. Most depressed persons don't have trouble getting sound sleep.

10. Eating enjoyment is essential in overcoming depression, even if it means gaining some weight.

ANSWERS

1. False. Most everyone can spot signs of depression, i.e., crying spells, poor appetite, general inertia, etc., but milder forms are much harder to recognize. Depression has been called the great masquerader for its symptoms appear in the guise of many other disturbances such as indigestion, fatigue, indifference and agitation, and a professional is usually needed to make a diagnosis here.

2. True. Poor diet, particularly one of junk foods like candy, sodas, potato chips, can trigger depressed moods. Also excess sugar in the bloodstream often leads to mood swings and inner tension.

Research under Dr. Regina Casper of the Illinois Psychiatric Institute in Chicago, shows that even salty foods which cause us to retain water and bring on a bloated feeling, will intensify depression.

3. False. Blood sugar tests often show changes in hormonal levels. Drs. Edward DeMet and Angelos Halaris of the University of Chicago, Brain Surgery Research Pavillion, developed a blood test which was given to over 60 depressed and manic patients at Michael Reese Hospital and Manteno State Hospital, both in Chicago. Results showed a relationship between blood elements and a patient's moods and response to treatment.

4. False. Emotional reactions to love loss can be quite disabling. Clinical depression of this type (called hysteroid dysphoria) in some cases, can even be life threatening. Typical victims are women, although men also suffer from it. It can be successfully treated with medications and psychotherapy.

5. False. Although we inherit biological patterns which involve hormones and enzymes in the brain, the major part of our reaction is based on how we perceive our situation and this determines just how we will feel about it.

6. False. Probably because of a more complex endocrine system twice as many women as men suffer from melancholy.

7. False. Alcohol, even in the smallest amounts, is a central nervous system depressant. Although we may experience a feeling of transient well being after a drink, when its effects wear off, we're apt to sink even lower into the dumps.

8. False. Exercise does reduce depression somewhat. The chief of psychiatry at San Diego's Mercy Hospital, uses jogging as therapy for many moderately depressed patients. He theorizes that this stimulates the release of endorphin, a brain secretion which promotes good feeling. It is believed that this is what happens when joggers hit a "high" after a period of prolonged running.

9. False. Most physicians recognize that insomnia is a very clear sign of depression. In addition, if a depressive does manage to fall asleep, it is usually a restless sleep.

10. True. Generally, any source of satisfaction is beneficial for a down-mood person, and this includes the pleasure of eating tasty food and drink.

SCORE

An average score on this depression quiz is at least 5 correct answers. A score over 5 suggests you might be slipping into a "blue funk" and you might find it helpful to talk with your doctor.

ARE YOU A SURVIVOR?

After the bloody French revolution of the late 18th century, a statesman of the newly formed government asked a weary peasant: "What constructive thing did you do during the great civil war?" His answer was brief: "Sir, I survived!" In the face of extreme adversity, merely surviving may indeed be the most heroic act.

Our news media bring daily reports of those who are suddenly plunged into desperate situations, but we seldom hear about how they cope with their lot after it has struck. Most survive, but some don't.

Independent research by Professors Salvatore Maddi of the University of Chicago and David McClelland of Harvard shows that survival in a crisis depends on a number of personal factors—a hardiness of spirit, resilience to stress and a positive attitude are all necessary to carry on in the face of adversity. Does this describe you?

How would you fare if you lost a loved one, a job, or your house, to mention just a few of life's traumas? To help you be objective about answering the items ahead, we won't reveal much more about the personality traits of survivors until after you've taken the quiz.

Answer each statement: Not True (NT); Somewhat True (ST); or Very True (VT) then read on for explanations.

1. I feel a sense of dedication to some aspect of my life (i.e., to my family, school, church, community, etc.).

2. I am satisfied with the rate of progress toward the goals I have set for myself.

3. It's better to be smart than lucky.

4. When good things happen they come about because of hard work.

5. People can get their own way if they just keep trying.

6. Once I make my mind up about something I usually don't change it

7. When I fail at a task, it usually weighs on my mind a long while.

Answer True or False to items 8-10

8. It's best to adapt as well as possible to setbacks in life because there's not much one can do to alter fate.

9. It has always been hard for me to adjust to life changes, (i.e., to a new job, school, neighborhood, etc.).

10. I usually find it hard to trust strangers and to build friendships.

EXPLANATION

As a group, survivors have certain personality traits in common and the quiz reflects them. These are:

1. There is a dedication and a purpose to their lives. A sense of involvement in something they are doing in life. A commitment to something (a person, a cause, a group). (Items 1, 2, 10)

2. A feeling of control over their life. A certitude that the outcomes in living are the direct result of their abilities and efforts. (Items 3, 4, 5)

3. The courage to be open to change. The self-confidence to face the unexpected and to make necessary adjustments. (Items 8, 9)

4. Persistence in the face of adversity. This is the drive to stay the course, even when things get tough. (Item 6)

In contrast to these favorable survivor qualities, McClelland found that persons most vulnerable to breakdown under heavy stress often have a high power drive (a need to be dominant over others) and a high degree of inhibition about expressing it. Such types may curb their power drive (assertiveness, aggressiveness, competitiveness, etc.) in a socially approved way, but all too often, they tend to become ineffectual or immobilized when adversity strikes.

An interesting post-trauma reaction of survivors was studied at Yale University in the early 1970s. It seems that some people can't come through a tragedy without suffering. (Item 7) It's called the "survivor syndrome" and it occurs when survivors develop guilt, depression and anxiety after they have emerged safely from a crisis while their loved ones or friends didn't.

SCORE

For items 1-7, take one point for each NT answer. Take 2 points for each ST answer. Take 3 points for each VT answer.

For items 8-10, take 1 point for each True answer and 3 points for each False answer.

Total your points and consider that:

25-30 points. You are an above average survivor with the resilience to carry on and be supportive of others if a crisis hits.

17-24 points. You are average in times of high stress and, though it may take somewhat longer than it would for a high scorer, you can cope with most setbacks.

16 or fewer points. You're vulnerable to adversity. Try to become more involved in a worthy life goal. Do things which will bring you a more positive, self-confident attitude.

ARE YOU LIVING ON THE EDGE? (WHAT'S YOUR RISK PROFILE?)

How much do you risk your physical or emotional health? General Health, Inc. (GHI), in Washington D.C. has health risk data on thousands of workers, compiled from numerous sources which may give you the answer.

GHI (not to be confused with Group Health Insurance, an HMO) provides personal risk health questionnaires to numerous civil and private employers as part of their health plan for workers to recognize the early signs of health failure. Some of their clients include the Ford Motor Company, ARCO oil, and New York State.

Ahead are items that may shed some light on whether or not you are living a pattern which portends a physical or emotional breakdown. They are adapted (with permission) from General Health, Inc.

Answer as follows: 1 for almost never, 2 for sometimes, and 3 for often.

1. Being the best in most things is important to me.
2. I try hard to win at games even if playing with children.
3. When waiting in ticket lines, at the supermarket, etc, I become very impatient.
4. When I am angry, I drive my car fast.
5. Most of my friends would consider me more aggressive than most people in going after what I want.
6. It makes me angry when I am kept waiting for an appointment or a date.
7. I enjoy competing very much.
8. When I see inefficiency in my co-workers or friends, it annoys me.
9. I need a drink or tranquilizer before I face tough situations.
10. I have physical symptoms like headaches, stomach cramps, and low back pain.
11. My sleep is restless and I have bad dreams.
12. In contrast to earlier times, I seem to be reluctant to meet new friends or go out socially.

SCORE

Total up your points and use this guide for what it means:

12-17 points. You are in a low risk category when it comes to developing a mental or physical breakdown.

18-26 points. You are in the average range compared with others in the general population.

27-36 points. You are in the high risk category when it comes to safeguarding your health. Your life pattern is extreme and if you continue on your present course, you may have a breakdown much before others who are of the same age.

NOTE: Learn to divide your goals into small achievable units, set priorities and let less important things wait. Allow more time for activity than is required. Don't feel rushed about life.

Dr. James E. Bernstein, president of GHI, who heads up a staff of more than 40 professionals in the health care and data retrieval fields, founded GHI in 1976. It draws on numerous sources for its data base such as the National Institute of Health and the Office of Health Information and Health Promotion of the US Department of Health and Health Services.

"Help!"

CHAPTER 9
ISSUES OF THE DAY

ARE YOU A ROAD HAZARD?

I recently took a defensive driver course and the first question the instructor asked was: "What is the main cause of highway accidents?" The answer may surprise you. Would you say weather conditions, mechanical failure, poor roads? If you picked one of these you'd be wrong.

Like the carpenter who botches a job then blames his tools, the careless driver often cites factors like: a rain storm, bad brakes, potholes, etc. to explain his mishaps. But the truth is that the primary cause of car accidents is, and has always been, human error through poor judgment and attitudes.

Consider this quiz to be most crucial for your survival. Be brutally honest in your answers, it might just save your life.

If you or someone you know has been having an unusual number of road mishaps, it's probably due to human error and our quiz is based on such errors. The quiz ahead may help.

Answer True or False:

1. Do you make it a habit to note what's happening on the road far ahead?

2. Do you often drive with one hand on the wheel?

3. Are you often late in getting to your destination because you didn't allow extra time?

4. If the driver ahead weaves or slows down as he approaches a corner, would you judge that he probably would turn?

5. Do you often make other drivers angry by a remark or gesture?

6. Before you take the wheel do you routinely unwind when emotionally upset (angry, anxious, depressed)?

7. Have others indicated that you have a short fuse with drivers who are slow to let you pass?

8. When driving, do you become more frustrated that most of your friends do?

9. In the daytime, do you put your lights on when using your windshield wipers?

10. Do you use a hand held cell phone when driving?

11. Are you often surprised by another vehicle suddenly appearing next to you?

12. Whenever practical, do you signal your slightest intentions to other drivers?

13. Does it happen that you must hit the brake hard more than two times in a month?

14. Do you make it a rule to keep a good distance from the driver who runs red lights or violates other road rules?

15. Are you wary of drivers with battered cars?

16. Do you always give pedestrians and cyclists the benefit of the doubt?

17. Are you often time-conscious when you drive; i.e., mindful about getting to your destination in a limited time span?

18. More than two times a month, are you surprised by a vehicle passing you that you were not aware of before?

19. Do other drivers show annoyance with your driving more than one or two times in a month?

20. Are you likely to speed up when the light changes to yellow to make it through an intersection before it changes to red?

SCORE

Take one point for each correct answer shown below.

1. True, 2. False, 3. False, 4. True, 5. False, 6. True, 7. False, 8. False, 9. True, 10. False, 11. False, 12. True, 13. False, 14. True, 15. True, 16. True, 17. False, 18. False, 19. False, 20. False.

EXPLANATION

What might you ask is the most common type of accident which leads to 60,000 deaths and 5 million injuries each year? The National Safety Council in Chicago, reports that it is: failure to yield right of way.

A large part of the time, failure to yield right of way is a personality quirk of some drivers with poor judgment, low empathy and lacking in habits of common courtesy. More often than not they could avoid danger by being less selfish, putting themselves in the other driver's spot and by just showing more respect for his rights.

WHAT YOUR SCORE MEANS

Consider a score of 16 or more to indicate you are a better than average driver. A score of less than 13 shows poor driver judgment. No matter what your score, there's always room for improvement. Keep these tips in mind:

1. If another car follows too closely, move and let it pass.

2. Stay out of the blind spot of other cars especially trucks, and continually check your own.

3. When in doubt, be more than willing to yield the right of way.

4. Avoid making left hand turns if at all possible.

5. When there is much activity ahead, expect that something unusual might occur and be prepared for the unexpected i.e., that something unusual might occur and be prepared for the unexpected.

Here's a useful acronym: S A F E

Safe speed. Always drive within the speed limit. Never drive out of control.

Allow. When in doubt, be more than willing to yield the right of way.

Follow. Always follow the vehicle ahead keeping at least one car length behind for every 10 miles per hour that you're moving.

Expect. Expect that your trip might take longer than you think. Give yourself a few more minutes than you need.

Part of the data and quiz were based on information from the Metropolitan Life Insurance Co. of NY, Exxon Corp., the 55-Alive Mature Driver Program of the American Association of Retired Persons and General Motors Corp.

ARE YOU CONSERVATIVE OR LIBERAL?

Every election year, the battle lines form between conservatives and liberals. In theory, socio-economic level is a clue to political party affiliation. The left is generally comprised of the lower working class, the liberals. On the right are the financially secure, the conservatives. In the center is the middle class, the moderates. But in practice there is much overlap among the groups.

There are many wealthy leftists just as there are working-class conservatives.

Voting patterns indicate much more than economic status. How we vote reflects more of our personality than we might realize.

Conservatism and liberalism are deep personality traits that correlate with other areas of a person's life, such as his religious beliefs, prejudices and social values.

One's political bent can even extend into stock-market behavior and to decisions about what to wear, what cars to drive and what television programs to watch. So, psychologically speaking, saying that you are a conservative or a liberal is saying a great deal.

A scale of conservatism was constructed in 1982 by Professor John Ray of the University of New South Wales in Australia. The scale was used with many American subjects and was found to be a reliable indicator of conservative and liberal attitudes. Ten items from this scale (which originally had 68 items) have been adapted with permission, for the following quiz.

To know just how conservative or liberal you are, answer each item true or false. Explanations follow.

1. School children should have plenty of discipline.

2. Pornographic literature should be prohibited from public sale.

3. People should be allowed to hold demonstrations in the streets without police interference.

4. The police deserve more pay and praise for the difficult job they do.

5. Government attempts to prevent people from using marijuana are unfair.

6. Laws against homosexuality are old-fashioned and wrong.

7. Busing children to schools out of their neighborhood is an infringement of individual rights.

8. People who show disrespect for their country's flag should be punished for it.

9. The right of strikers to picket a firm should be protected.

10. Compulsory military training is unfair and has a tendency to make people belligerent.

EXPLANATION

Conservatives tend to cling to traditional patterns of living. They are wary of change and, as law-and-order personalities, they tend to uphold and defend the rules made by the establishment.

They are usually found at the upper end of the socioeconomic scale. They seek a structured environment, while liberals lobby for freedom from constraints.

Women tend to be more conservative than men in their actions and beliefs. Professionals tend to be more conservative than non-professionals and those who work for the government are the most moderate elements in a society and tend to vote conservative.

In the work world, executives in big business are more conservative than executives in small business and blue-collar workers tend to be somewhat more conservative than white-collar workers. Even within the blue-collar class, skilled workers tend to be more conservative than unskilled workers.

Conservative or liberal-minded personalities are formed in childhood and our parents, of course, strongly influence the direction our attitudes will take.

SCORE

Items 1, 2, 4, 7, 8 tend to be answered true by conservatives; the rest (3, 5, 6, 9, 10 are answered true by liberals.

Give yourself 1 point for each of your responses that correspond with the following key: 1. T, 2. T, 3. F, 4. T, 5. F, 6. F, 7. T, 8. T, 9. F, 10. F. (The key indicates how a conservative would answer the quiz.)

8-10 pts. You have strong conservative attitudes about life.

4-7 points. You are a moderate and have a balance between conservative and liberal attitudes.

0-3 points. You're high liberal

DO YOU SUFFER FROM SPRING FEVER?

There's hardly a poet who hasn't rhapsodized about the beauty of the season and about spring-time love. But a spring-fever romance or "a robin on the wing" tells only part of the story of this little-understood season as far as our psyches are concerned. For centuries, scientists have noted that the seasons influence our well being in many ways. However, a more exact-ing approach to the subject is a new science called biometeorology which started in Europe.

Studies in biometeorology have verified that seasonal changes have varied influences on our health. Did you know, for example, that glaucoma is more prevalent in winter than in summer, or that children grow more rapidly in spring than in any other season, or that appendicitis attacks are more frequent in summer than in winter?

Biometeorology has also uncovered interesting facts about how the seasons influence our mental and emotional makeup.

The following quiz tests your notions about the facts and fictions related to the spring season and its affect on behavior. The items are based on biometeorology research.

Answer true or false to each item, and then compare your views with the answers given in the key.

1. People are generally less nervous and irritable in spring than in any other season.

2. Criminal behavior is higher in spring than in any other season.

3. More people have mental breakdowns in spring than in other seasons.

4. Your child will have a higher IQ if born in spring than in any other season.

5. Your ability to react quickly, and thus avoid an accident, is keener in spring than in other seasons.

6. It's a myth that a baby's sex is influenced by the season of its birth.

7. Because it is the time of nature's reawakening, the suicide rate is lower in spring than in any other season.

8. Accuracy in work tends to increase during spring compared to other seasons.

9. Romance is more prevalent in spring than in other seasons.

10. More people of prominence are born in the spring than in other seasons.

EXPLANATION

1. False. Balmy weather seems to bring emotional unrest and mood swings. S.W. Tromp, author of *Medical Biometeorology*, collected data that showed that what poets call the "merry month of May" is in fact the month in which people experience the most disagreement and discord.

2. True. Each year, national statistics show that spring brings with it the highest number of crimes committed in nearly all categories.

3. True. Mental hospitals throughout the world report more admissions during the spring than during other seasons. A survey by Dr. C. Willmann of Heidelberg, Germany, disclosed that of the 13,500 patients he studied, more were admitted to hospitals in the spring than at other times.

4. False. In independent studies, psychologists Florence Goodenough and Clarence Mills confirmed that schoolchildren born in summer average slightly higher IQs than those born in cooler seasons. Some theorize that the basis for this is better fetal brain development during the warmer months.

5. False. Surveys of studies done by Tromp show that in spring our reaction time lengthens, thus we are not as quick to react to emergencies. Car and industrial accident rates are higher in spring than at other times in the year.

6. False. Although more male babies than female babies are born in summer, fall and winter, just the reverse is true in spring. There are significantly more girls than boys born between March and June.

7. False. Worldwide the suicide rate is higher in spring than in other seasons. In addition, William Peterson, author of *Man, Weather and Sun*, reports, somewhat incredibly perhaps, that not only is the suicide rate up but that tall, thin persons tend to commit suicide at the beginning of spring; stocky individuals later on.

8. False. Possibly because of glandular changes, we tend to lose accuracy in spring. In his book, *How Atmospheric Conditions Affect Your Health*, Michel Gauguelin reports that one study done in Holland, which ran over a year, found that the work accuracy of a group of chemical analysts declined significantly throughout the spring.

9. True. Love and mating activity in both man and animal tends to increase significantly during spring. Some endocrinologists call it the "spring hormonal crisis," when glandular activity increases. The endocrine glands are closely related to our romantic and sexual behavior.

10. True. Social scientist Ellsworth Huntington studied a sample of 1,210 notable people and found more born in early spring than in other seasons. Another survey of those listed in *Who's Who in America* showed similar results.

CAN PORN HURT YOU?

The pornography industry thrives. Unwanted exposure to porn has been growing. A recent study in the journal *Pediatrics*, shows that the viewing of Internet pornography by kids aged 10 to 17 has jumped from 25 percent in 2000, to 34 percent today. Researchers at The University of New Hampshire, Crimes Against Children Research Center (CACRC), call these findings disturbing.

It reports that 42% of US 10-to-17-year-olds said they'd been exposed to online pornography in the past year, and 66% of that group reported unwanted exposure. Each year obscene matter (films, books, pictures, etc.) grosses an estimated $9 billion. The Postmaster General finds that between 75-90 percent of all such material winds up in the hands of minors.

Also, evidence from research, such as that done at Stanford University in California shows that violence and sex do indeed have undesirable effects on the personality of children.

What are your thoughts on the subject? Mark Agree or Disagree to the following items, then read on.

1. Morality is not something which should be legislated.

2. Obscenity is in the eye of the beholder. He who believes something is evil will see it.

3. Freedom of expression is protected by the First Amendment and allows anyone to sell obscene material to any age group.

4. Obscenity is a victimless crime.

5. When consenting adults view obscene movies, no one is being, harmed.

6. Since the porno industry is flourishing it proves that Americans have a need for it.

7. If you don't want to view off-color movies on cable TV, turn the dial.

8. If you don't like porno material, don't buy it, but don't interfere with others' right to use it.

ANSWERS:

Some might consider the above to be clichés, others will see them as valid arguments in favor of present laws on pornography. Here are answers compiled by Morality in Media, a national anti-porn group in New York City.

1. Every law, to some degree, legislates morality by setting standards for its citizens. Each person must ultimately make the moral decision to obey or disobey.

2. The implication here is that obscenity is subjective. It is objective in the sense that it describes or depicts specific sexual activity that is prohibited by law to protect the common good.

3. Expressing ourselves is certainly protected by the First Amendment, but, in addition, the Supreme Court has said that obscenity is not protected any more than are libel or slander.

4. There is probably no such thing as a victimless crime. In porn sales, purchasers could be the immediate victims. The law argues that for each such victim, the moral fabric of society is diminished. A glaring instance of victimization in obscenity is children used in child pornography.

5. The Supreme Court decision of June 1973, disagreed with this notion stating: "We categorically disapprove the theory that obscene films acquire constitutional immunity simply because they are exhibited for consenting adults only. Rights and interests other than those of the advocates are involved i.e., the quality of life, the total community environment, the tone of commerce and, possibly, the public safety itself."

6. Like any product, the fact that some people want it makes it profitable. But surveys show that most Americans are vehemently opposed to porn and want it stopped. Often, however, they are discouraged in the face of a highly efficient industry, about 90 percent of which is controlled by organized crime.

7. Again the Court said the burden should not be on the TV viewer. In 1978 it ruled that the "turn the dial" argument does not hold up since a viewer may already have been assaulted. It declared that it's like running from a mugger after you've been attacked.

8. What you do is your business but your privacy right does not extend to the marketplace. Society does not want porn to pollute the environment in which we raise our children and it is illegal to exhibit obscenity to the public at large.

Scoring Key

MM grades all items as false.

Score

Take 1 point for each false answer.

6-8 pts.-You strongly concur with **MM**

3-5 pts.-You are average in agreement with **MM**

0-2 pts.-You mostly disagree with **MM** on these issues

Morality in Media is a non-profit organization founded by clergymen in 1962. It is a powerful lobby group which established the National Obscenity Law Center, a clearinghouse of legal information for attorneys.

WILL YOU KEEP THOSE NEW YEAR'S RESOLUTIONS?

It can't be more apparent that on January 1st "hope springs eternal in the human breast." That's the day you're likely to shudder when looking back on the past year's promises you made to yourself. Perhaps, you optimistically, think forward to the new year with a vow to turn over a new leaf.

But do you have what it takes to follow through on your pledges? The quiz below identifies some personality traits that may predict how you'll fare in the year ahead. Answer each item true or false. Be honest!

1. I usually delay doing an unpleasant chore.

2. I usually leave the drudgery of long-range planning to another family member.

3. I am known to be impulsive in my decision-making.

4. Most of my troubles are of my own doing.

5. A New Year's resolution is a private matter. It should be made only to yourself or a close friend.

6. Most people are too easy on themselves when it comes to making New Year's resolutions.

7. I have a talent for handling children, leading or teaching others or training animals.

8. New Year's Day is no different from any other time of the year for my resolving to change.

9. A person who is truly dedicated to achievement won't be bothered by fear of success.

10. I believe it's better to be lucky than to be smart.

11. I usually have to be pressured to achieve difficult tasks.

12. Highly successful people of average intelligence get to where they are because of some lucky breaks.

EXPLANATION

1. False. Putting things off is the mark of a procrastinator. Chances are the same personality traits will operate against you as you attempt to keep those New Year's resolutions.

2. False. Planning is essential to making progress. If you tend to shy away from making plans, you're less likely to reach your goals than someone who takes on the challenge. Planners build mental steps toward goals they pursue; this gives them drive to carry through to the end.

3. False. Persons who act on impulse usually regret it later. Although well intentioned, they make poor choices because they don't know themselves well enough to predict whether they'll be happy or able to live with a decision.

4. True. This is a favorite item on many personality tests. It indicates an inner-directed personality type, i.e., one who takes major responsibility for his or her destiny.

5. True. If we break a pledge to ourselves or even one close to us, we usually can excuse it without much regret. But breaking promises to several others is harder to deal with since there's the added element of social guilt or embarrassment. Behaviorists call it "social facilitation."

6. False. The opposite is true. When subjects in goal-setting experiments are asked to set levels of aspiration for themselves, they usually pick goals that are too high, and thereby unreachable.

7. True. Studies show that persons with these traits usually have dominance and perseverance in the things they attempt. As a group, they tend to keep more of their New Year's pledges than others.

8. False. New Year's Day presents a unique climate for making resolutions. There's a strong social awareness and participation in the tradition. All of this gives you an everyone's-doing-it psychological momentum that isn't there at any other time of the year.

9. False. Studies at the U.S. Office of Naval Research show that some achievers fear success. You may be as afraid of success in your resolutions as you are of failure, and therefore make an unconscious effort to defeat yourself. Dr. Leon Tec, author of *The Fear of Success*, has found that we may secretly wish to fail in our resolve because of the changes that may be brought about, such as added responsibility, if we succeed.

10. False. If you place more belief in luck or on outside factors rather than on your inner strength, it shows you are leaving the responsibility for your success to fate.

11. False. If you need outside pressure to operate at your best, it will work against you. Ultimately, keeping your New Year's resolutions will depend on the pressure you generate from within yourself to carry you through to victory.

12. False. This answer is similar to item 11. It's very rare that luck will make you a winner. Don't count on it. Unswerving determination is what leads to success.

SCORE

Take 1 point for each correct answer.

9-12 correct. You are very persevering and your high goal-orientation should help you to keep most of your New Year's resolutions.

4-8 correct. You have an average degree of determination to keep your pledges. You'll win some, lose some, but on the whole, you'll be happy that you made the effort.

0-3 correct. You'll have a rough time keeping your resolutions this year. Carefully review the promises you've made and be realistic about making progress and setting new goals. The trick for you is to be more practical and less idealistic about your next year goals.

DO YOUR XMAS GIFTS TELL ON YOU?

Christmas giving is a hallowed tradition, and practically everybody gets into a dither trying to find the right gifts for the right people at the right price. In the process, the common experience of Christmas shopping brings out many traits that aren't so noticeable during the rest of the year. In fact, psychologists have pointed out that gift- giving behavior can reveal important facets of your personality.

Experts also point out that your attitude, with or without a lot of money to spend, is indicative of your feelings about the whole holiday scene. The way you handle the problems of gift giving also reflects your attitude about giving pleasure to others.

The following quiz describes typical behavior patterns that often distinguish the joyous giver from the grumpy giver. The questions, though not part of a standardized test, are based on behavior patterns observed in many people from all walks of life.

Answer each question YES or NO to find out the degree of your Christmas spirit.

1. Do you buy more expensive gifts for richer friends or relatives than you do for poorer ones?
2. Have you recycled a gift giving someone a present you received but didn't like or already have?
3. Do you enjoy giving gifts more than receiving them?
4. Do you buy quantities of the same gift item and give each of them to different individuals?
5. Do you feel Christmas gift giving is overdone and should be minimized?
6. Are you a repeat giver, in that you annually give some people the same gift, such as a bottle of scotch, a tie, a box of candy?
7. Do you usually cram most of your shopping into the last few days before Christmas?
8. Do you play the waiting game when undecided about giving someone a gift, taking your cue from whether that person gives you a gift first?
9. Do you often wind up giving cash because you didn't want to bother to shop?
10. Do you think gift certificates tend to be a cop-out?

ANSWERS

1. No, 2. No, 3. Yes, 4. No, 5. No, 6. No, 7. No, 8. No, 9. No, 10. Yes.

SCORE

Give yourself 1 point for each answer that corresponds with those given in the answer key.

8 or more points. You are generally mindful of others' needs and have a positive attitude toward them. You probably enjoy good Christmas cheer in exchanging gifts and have more fun at holiday gatherings than the average person. You are a happy giver most of the time.

4 to 7 points. Although you are generally concerned with the needs of others, you slip up now and then. Your Christmas spirit is fair, and though you look forward to holiday get-togethers, if you missed one it wouldn't bother you very much. You, too, are a happy giver, though less so than a higher scorer.

3 or fewer points. You tend to see holiday gift-giving as a drain on time, energy and money. You'd have to work hard at being a good giver or receiver. If you had your druthers, you'd probably want to skip the non-religious holiday atmosphere altogether.

NOTE

Some interesting findings:

A 2005 survey showed that four out of five Americans think the holidays are too materialistic, according to the Center for a New American Dream, which promotes responsible consumption.

Research by Margaret Rucker, a consumer psychologist at the University of California, Davis, found that men are typically more price-conscious and practical when it comes to the gifts they give and get, while women tend to be more concerned about giving and receiving gifts with emotional significance.

DO YOU SUFFER FROM SANTA SYNDROME?

Christmas is a time when some of us fall prey to a chronic seasonal malady called "spending fever." The symptoms can be self-diagnosed: swelling (of the shopping list), distorted vision (eyes that are larger than one's budget), and chills (due to cold cash in the pocket).

Actually, spending fever isn't just a seasonal bug. It persists throughout the year, but during the holidays the resistance of its victims drops sharply as they become even more susceptible to its sting.

The roots of the disorder are psychological. Herb Goldberg and Robert Lewis, California psychologists and authors of *Money Madness*, call the compulsive spender a "love buyer." They sum up the condition succinctly: "The essence of the love buyer's Santa Claus syndrome is that by bestowing gifts on all the deserving people in the world, he expects to receive their undying love and devotion." Actually, the spender who can't fight the temptation to buy also spends money on himself. It is the same process in reverse: "I buy (and hoard) love for myself."

Do you know of someone who fits this description or do you see a glimpse of yourself here? To learn if you are vulnerable to spending fever, take the following quiz. It is based on the findings of Goldberg and Lewis.

Answer each item as follows: 1. rarely or never; 2. occasionally; 3. often.

1. I return from a store with more items than I'd planned to buy.
2. When I shop, I take several credit cards or plenty of cash along so I won't run short.
3. My family or I don't get much use out of the things buy.
4. When I admire something that a friend has bought, I go out and buy the item too.
5. The more money I have, the more I tend to spend.
6. I enjoy going to big sales.
7. Spending money is a way to boost my morale when I feel blue.
8. I enjoy telling friends about my bargain purchases.

9. When I spot something I need or something that is very appealing, I buy it immediately without bothering to do much comparison shopping.

10. When I buy something personal, like jewelry or clothes, I'm more mindful of how it will impress others than with how much I really need it.

SCORE

To tally your score, add the numbers of your responses to the quiz items. If you scored:

10-17 points. You have good control over your spending impulses, but do try to avoid being too tight-fisted when it comes to being good to yourself or others, or you'll become a modern-day Scrooge.

18-23 points. You're an average spender with enough flexibility to blow a few dollars now and then for a special occasion.

24-30 points. You suffer from spending fever. But before you open a chapter of Overspenders Anonymous in your neighborhood, here are some helpful guidelines:

1. Use a shopping list.
2. Never shop when upset or blue.
3. Carry a limited amount of cash and no credit cards.
4. Shop with a friend (preferably one who is a low scorer on the quiz).

EXPLANATION

Freudians tell us that as a child the compulsive spender felt insecure about his parents' love, and searched for ways to obtain their approval. As he grew older he came to view money as power, and used it as a tool for winning others' loyalty and gaining their admiration.

Conspicuous spenders are often "moneyphobes." It makes them feel uncomfortable (phobic) to accumulate cash in their pockets, and they feel relieved when it's spent. Although society fosters the attitude that money should be spent wisely and that we should feel guilty when we "throw it away," compulsive spenders have not mastered the task of wise money management. To them, owning money means having a grown-up responsibility to use it wisely, and they avoid doing so.

Such types often pay the whole check when at a restaurant with friends, buy impractical items for their homes and usually own a number of like items, such as computer gadgets, hairdryers, etc., when one would suffice.

So, if you buy impulsively, spend money on extravagant gifts for loved ones, and always seem to be the one who volunteers to pay for that last round of drinks at the bar, examine your spending habits. This may be the year to resolve that your purchases should have sound reasoning behind them, and that the money you put away, however small the amount, can one day be blown on something you really, really want,

WHAT SECRET ATTITUDES DO KIDS HARBOR ABOUT POLICE?

In Philadelphia, two patrol cars sent to arrest a murder suspect, were met with rocks and bottles hurled by angry teens. The scene, which could have happened in many American cities, is testimony that some youths aren't reluctant about acting out their hostility toward the police.

In one of the most meaningful studies on the subject of youth's perception of the law, the late Dr. Robert Fortune, head of secondary education at the University of Cincinnati, surveyed the attitudes of boys and girls between the ages of 12 and 16 and came to some startling conclusions. These are summarized in his book, *Changing Juvenile Attitudes Toward Police.*

The quiz ahead is based on his findings. To find out where you stand on the subject, answer True or False to the items. Explanations follow.

1. As a child matures, his attitudes about police change for the better.

2. Attitudes toward police vary with socio-economic level, with kids from lower levels showing more respect toward them than those from higher levels.

3. Teens differ according to gender: girls have a more favorable reaction to cops than do boys.

4. Compared with a generation ago, teenagers today have a better understanding and acceptance of a law officer's job because of the media.

5. Attitudes about criminal justice are fairly consistent from one ethnic group to another.

6. Even if a young person goes to church it won't influence what he/she thinks about police.

7. Belligerent feelings toward the law cut across all levels of scholastic competence.

8. Schools are increasingly helping to promote favorable attitudes toward police.

9. A youngster's views of police are influenced more by their parents than by their peer group.

10. A teenager is more likely to show defiance of police when in a group than when he/she is alone.

EXPLANATION

1. False. Unfortunately, this isn't always the case. Youngsters in 9th grade showed significantly worse attitudes compared with when they were in 7th grade.

2. False. The lower a juvenile's socio-economic level, the more negative is his/her attitude toward the police.

3. True. Girls do have better attitudes toward law officers than boys do.

4. False. Although the media is a powerful tool for education, thus far it hasn't shown to improve teenage relations with police.

5. False. A number of studies have supported Fortune's finding that minority group kids as well as adults, show more distrust of police than those from majority groups.

6. False. Boys who are regular churchgoers tend to have more favorable notions about law officers than do those who don't attend church. On the other hand, girls who attend church have the same attitudes as girls who do not.

7. False. Acceptance does go along with doing well at school. Good students tend to accept police more than those who are faring poorly.

8. False. Fortune's research, national in scope, found that, unfortunately, few curricula include programs to promote positive perceptions of law officers.

9. False. Fortune's results support that of others who learned that teen peers are even more powerful an influence than their parents.

10. True. But on the other hand, he/she is more likely to help a victim in need if alone rather than when with peers.

Fortune and his associates, discovered that not only were young people "ignorant of the nature of the law and the mission of law enforcement" but that "police officers who had initial contacts with these youths, were themselves ignorant of the nature of early adolescence".

With his premise that ignorance of others often breeds animosity toward them, he established the Center for Law Related Education. Here youngsters learn about police functions in a 6-week program, in which they ask plenty of questions as they tour local police headquarters, ride for a night in an unmarked squad car, etc. In every instance boys and girls significantly altered their attitudes for the better. Those in the control groups (where no courses were given) did not change their views or grew more hostile toward police and the criminal justice system. Fortune convinced Ohio officials to provide programs throughout the state and, later, federal funding made the curriculum available to such states as California, Florida, New York, and Arkansas, where equally good results were obtained

SCORE
Give yourself 1 point for each correct answer. A score of 5 or 6 shows an average grasp of how teens view police. Keep in mind two important points; (1) if you are in contact with youngsters, your views may influence their thinking about police, but, and even more significant, (2) their friends might just override you.

WHAT IS PMS ANYWAY?
Each month many women become achy, listless, fatigued, and despondent. Some even become violent and paranoid. The disorder that causes such mood swings and discomfort is called premenstrual syndrome (PMS). 50 to 75 percent of all women of childbearing age suffer from PMS in varying degrees.

The malady, brought on by monthly changes in the hormonal balance of the reproductive system, was, until recently, a condition tolerated by its sufferers and largely ignored by physicians who told women their symptoms were all in their minds.

Many medical experts believe that PMS is caused by an imbalance of the estrogen-progesterone hormone ratio in the bloodstream. But new evidence suggests that a crucial role might be played by neurotransmitters – brain hormones that carry signals between nerves. These hormones trigger the release of chemicals that often bring on symptoms of PMS.

Although PMS is strictly an illness of women, it also has powerful ripple effects on others. Every man or boy who has ever coped with a combative girlfriend, a weepy sister or an otherwise sweet mother turned harsh, is affected by the personality changes that PMS sometimes brings about.

The following quiz may provide some understanding of this complex affliction for both women who suffer from it and for those in their lives who must share their distress. The quiz is based on research done at The Johns Hopkins University in Baltimore, Md., where a non-drug therapy, which incorporates vitamins and exercise, is being studied, and the National Institute of Mental Health in Bethesda, Md., which is conducting the largest study ever done on PMS and its psychological impact. How much do you know about PMS?

Answer "true" or "false" for each item. Then read on for explanations.

1. Signs of PMS usually start 24 to 48 hours before a woman's period.

2. Medical authorities now know the cause of PMS and have a cure for it.

3. Because so much is said about PMS (in the press, TV, etc.), it's relatively easy for a woman to diagnose her own condition.

4. Many therapies, including vitamin therapy, are suggested for PMS, but none seems to help.

5. For the most part, all PMS patients suffer from the same symptoms—nausea, fatigue, irritability, cramps, etc.

6. If you're under 21, you need not worry much about getting PMS.

7. Hormone treatments have been shown to help PMS sufferers.

8. Because PMS produces such erratic reactions, physicians are reluctant to give patients responsibility in managing their symptoms.

9. You shouldn't exercise or do strenuous activities during your period.

10. PMS is curable.

EXPLANATION

All items are false.

1. Symptoms begin gradually after ovulation, about two weeks before a period, but they stop 24 to 48 hours before the onset of menstruation itself.

2. To date, there is no cure for PMS, only measures for symptom relief.

3. Experts do not recommend self-diagnosis. Consult your gynecologist, who will probably ask you to chart your day-to-day symptoms so that an effective treatment program can be outlined for you.

4. Dr. Robert London, director of clinical research at Sinai Hospital in Baltimore, Md., has concluded studies that show that vitamin therapy (using vitamins B6 and E) can be of great value for women with PMS. His findings have been verified by other scientists.

5. There are four basic sets of symptoms of PMS: 1. nervous tension, mood swings and anxiety; 2. weight gain, swelling of extremities and abdominal bloating; 3. headache, increased appetite (especially for sweets) and fainting; 4. depression and insomnia. (There can be an overlapping of the groups; it can also vary from month to month.)

6. PMS can begin at puberty (age 12 to 13) and last until menopause (age 45 to 55), but it is most common in the 30- to 45-year-old group.

7. Progesterone has been approved by the U.S. Food and Drug Administration for use in treating PMS It is used to treat some cases.

8. At Johns Hopkins University, where the first non-drug approach to PMS has been devised, patients are told to follow this four-step program of self-management: (1) Exercise for one-half hour twice daily; (2) Eat plenty of protein and few carbohydrates; (3) Take vitamin E daily and vitamin B6 only on symptom days; (4) Take some time to unwind and relax each day.

9. Menstruation is a normal function. Your period is not a disability, you can do anything during your period that you can do when you're not menstruating. Once treated as a time when women were "sick," menstruating women rested, stayed home, and didn't socialize.

10. As long as the ovaries produce eggs, PMS symptoms can occur. When this cycle is interrupted, during pregnancy and at menopause, women generally report that the condition goes away. Those who undergo a total hysterectomy, in which both ovaries are removed, also experience a cessation of symptoms. Research into vitamin deficiencies, chemical imbalances and stress reduction continues.

SCORE
Women should get at least 6 correct on this quiz, men perhaps slightly less.

The quiz is as much a vehicle for conveying facts on PMS as it is a scale to gauge your knowledge of it. If you're a woman who suffers from PMS perhaps the quiz items provided new information on how to cope with it. If you are not a PMS sufferer the quiz could be a step toward better understanding of women who are afflicted with it.

ONE FINAL WORD
Any author who braves writing a quiz book becomes a target for critics who chant,

"it's not valid enough to take seriously etc." But remember a quiz or test, is just a small sample of a reality under our focus. It's not a complete heavily documented probe, like a research protocol or questionnaire. If that were our goal, readers would be turned off, dulled into boredom. It doesn't have the statistical baggage, which a full-blown protocol might have. But it can be useful in giving a quick probe into a trait and offer a glimpse into a part of our personality, which perhaps we've never thought much about before.

Salvatore V. Didato, PhD is a clinical psychologist and has been a television, newspaper and radio commentator on human affairs. He is the author of *Psychotechniques* and has developed a number of behavior modification techniques that have proved effective in treating habit disturbances like smoking, insomnia, and eating disorders as well as phobias and depressive symptoms

His articles have been published in numerous periodicals including *Parade, Harper's Bazaar, Cosmopolitan, The New York Times, Brides, Self, Good Housekeeping, Family Weekly,* and *Reader's Digest* (Canada). His behavior essays have been syndicated by The Gannett News Service, King Features, Syndication Sales Co., United Press International, and others.

His column "BEHAVIOR BEHIND THE NEWS" won him a commendation from the American Psychological Association for "outstanding reporting on the field of psychology" and in 1980, Dr. Didato was granted the "Outstanding Psychologist of the Year" award by the Westchester County Psychological Association of New York.

He is the author of *The Big Book of Personality Tests* (Black Dog & Leventhal, 2003), which has sold over 140,000 copies and is printed in 10 foreign editions.

17563998R00106

Made in the USA
San Bernardino, CA
15 December 2014